NO LONGER PROPERTY OF
ANYTHINK LIBRARIES/
RANGEVIEW LIBRARY DISTRICT

HOW TO LEAD OTHERS

D0843738

Praise for *How to Lead Others*

"This book is a must read for anybody in a leadership role. It is entertaining, thought-provoking and clear, providing an invaluable source of guidance from a humble, acutely observant, wise and internationally-renowned scholar."

Sir Laurie Magnus, Chairman, Windsor Leadership Trust

"Whatever stage you've reached in your personal leadership journey, this book is provocative, challenging and invaluable. Using a skilful blend of observation, analysis, storytelling and exercises, John Adair provokes healthy self-examination. Unlike many books on leadership, it's also a cracking read."

Christopher Rodrigues CBE, Chairman, British Council

"Management has Peter Drucker. **But Leadership has John Adair.** With his customary clear style, John Adair has created a simple, easy-to-follow text which will allow any leader from novice to those with years of experience to become more effective. Guidance is through straightforward text, powerful exercises and thorough check-lists. It's a fast read but one with all the depth you need."

**Nicholas Bate, Founder, Strategic Edge;
author of 20 books on leadership**

"It was from Professor John Adair that I first learned that leadership is a verb. *How to Lead Others* is full of practical tips and exercises underpinned by John's inimitable wisdom. Read this book reflectively as a source of inspiration and guidance for your own journey as a leader."

Georgina Noakes, Founder and Director, Brightside

"John has written a practical guide to leadership brought beautifully to life by quotes drawn from many cultures and moments in time. At its heart he reinforces the critical importance for any aspiring leader to relentlessly build shared purpose, to earn respect and always be a leader for good."

**Emma Fitzgerald, Managing Director
Wholesale Operations, Severn Trent plc**

HOW TO LEAD OTHERS

OTHERS

Eight lessons for beginners

JOHN ADAIR

BLOOMSBURY BUSINESS

LONDON • NEW YORK • OXFORD • NEW DELHI • SYDNEY

BLOOMSBURY BUSINESS
Bloomsbury Publishing Plc
50 Bedford Square, London, WC1B 3DP, UK
1385 Broadway, New York, NY 10018, USA

BLOOMSBURY, BLOOMSBURY BUSINESS and the Diana logo are
trademarks of Bloomsbury Publishing Plc

First published in Great Britain 2019

Copyright © John Adair, 2019
Cover design by Emma J Hardy

John Adair has asserted his right under the Copyright, Designs and Patents Act,
1988, to be identified as Author of this work.

All rights reserved. No part of this publication may be reproduced or transmitted
in any form or by any means, electronic or mechanical, including photocopying,
recording, or any information storage or retrieval system, without prior
permission in writing from the publishers.

Bloomsbury Publishing Plc does not have any control over, or responsibility for,
any third-party websites referred to or in this book. All internet addresses given
in this book were correct at the time of going to press. The author and publisher
regret any inconvenience caused if addresses have changed or sites have ceased
to exist, but can accept no responsibility for any such changes.

A catalogue record for this book is available from the British Library.

Library of Congress Cataloging-in-Publication Data
Names: Adair, John Eric, 1934– author.
Title: How to lead others : seven lessons for beginners / John Adair.
Description: New York : Bloomsbury Publishing Plc, [2018] | Includes
bibliographical references and index.
Identifiers: LCCN 2018021274 (print) | LCCN 2018021821 (ebook) |
ISBN 9781472956989 (ePUB) | ISBN 9781472956965 (ePDF) |
ISBN 9781472956996 (eXML) | ISBN 9781472956972 (Paperback)
Subjects: LCSH: Leadership.
Classification: LCC HD57.7 (ebook) | LCC HD57.7 .A27494 2018 (print) |
DDC 658.4/092—dc23
LC record available at https://lccn.loc.gov/2018021274

ISBN: PB: 978-1-4729-5697-2
         ePDF: 978-1-4729-5696-5
         eBook: 978-1-4729-5698-9

Typeset by RefineCatch Limited, Bungay, Suffolk
Printed and bound Great Britain

To find out more about our authors and books visit www.bloomsbury.com
and sign up for our newsletters.

CONTENTS

Introduction

You are not born a leader, you become one.

A PROVERB OF THE BAMILEKE PEOPLE IN WEST AFRICA

Welcome to this book! I am assuming that you have a direct personal interest in leadership. You may be already in a position which you suspect – or have been told – requires leadership. You may perhaps be an experienced leader, or you may be on the threshold of a career in management in which you will be expected to become a leader. In each case, leadership matters to you. Whatever your situation, this book is designed to help you to improve your leadership ability. *When they call you a reaper, sharpen your scythe.*

My particular focus throughout is upon you and the fledgling leader, the beginner, in the art of leading others. I can well remember personally it can be daunting to say the least to be facing the prospect of becoming leader of a team in the work environment for the first time. At least some of its members could be older and more experienced than you are. How do you acquire their respect? How do you become credible?

The way ahead

In PART ONE, Understanding Leadership, I shall share with you the story of how mankind has come to acquire a body of knowledge about leadership. The 'jewel in the crown' of that knowledge is the discovery of the generic role of *leader*. That in turn stemmed from a groundbreaking discovery about the nature of all working groups.

If you can understand clearly that generic role – and inscribe it on the retina of your eye – you will be halfway to becoming an effective leader.

The generic role of leader can be further broken down into **functions**. PART TWO, Developing Your Leadership Skills, takes you into the territory of turning these functions into your personal and professional skills. This set of eight functions should be taken as indicative and open-ended, but all the most important ones are there.

How to use this book

In order to get the most from this book it is best to read it through once to get a general understanding. Then go back and work through the checklist questions and exercises. If you can persuade a friend or colleague to check your answers, so much the better.

Do not assume that you have to start from the beginning and read through to the end. The book is organized to move from the general to the more particular, from the whole to the specific part. Some people, however, prefer to learn by starting off with the particular (e.g. drills, skills or techniques) and moving to general. If you belong to this group it may be better for you to start with Part Two and work hard on that and then read Part One.

You may also, for example, prefer to complete the **checklists** at the end of most chapters *before* reading the chapter rather than afterwards. Decide your strategy for using the book now, according to your depth of interest and preferred method of learning.

The summary of **key points** at the end of each chapter is designed as a succinct *aide-memoire*, but occasionally I throw in a new idea just to see if you are still awake!

How we learn

Regardless of which approach you adopt or how carefully you read this book, you will learn nothing about leadership unless you make a conscious effort to relate the points to your real-life experience. It is essential to bear in mind that people learn by the interaction of

PRINCIPLES	$\longrightarrow$	EXPERIENCE
or	and	or
THEORY	$\longleftarrow$	PRACTICE

It is when sparks jump between these two poles – the general and the actual – that learning occurs. So you need both. The various case studies and examples in this book are designed to be 'stepping stones':

PRINCIPLES $\longrightarrow$ THIRD-PERSON $\longrightarrow$ *YOUR*
EXAMPLES EXPERIENCE

Equally, the process must work in reverse. Your practical knowledge, gleaned from both observation of actual leaders and your own practical experience, must be brought to bear in a constructively critical way on the ideas presented in this book.

For the essentials of leadership – the qualities, functions and principles – are the same for any field of work. I am assuming that you have sufficient creative intelligence to search for lessons about leadership in areas other than your own work sphere. To become an educated leader as well as a trained one you need a *'wide span of relevance'*. There will be a *principle* or general method in these examples from history or another field which is relevant to you. You have to identify that principle with my help and *transfer* or translate it to the context of your own field.

So read the book reflectively. Put it down occasionally and work on some incidents in your own career which are illuminated by the book, since personal reflections will illustrate leadership lessons better than any secondhand case study.

The value of having some principles, guidelines or checklists of leadership is that they will cut down the time you take to learn from experience. As Henry Ford said, 'By the time a man is ready to graduate from the University of Experience he is too old to work!' George Bernard Shaw added that the fees you have to pay in that hard school are exceptionally high. At least I hope to spare you some of that expense!

*   *   *   *   *

As with most things in life, the more you put into reading, marking and inwardly digesting the following pages, the more you will get out of them.

Search this book as you may, you never find me saying that leadership is easy. It is simple but not easy. Yet, if you stay the course, I promise that you will find being a leader in your field immensely rewarding. Are you up for the challenge?

The true conclusion

In the list of Contents, you may notice that there is no Conclusion. There is a real reason for this absence: I see you as my partner in writing this book. It is up to you to write its conclusion in your own life and work as a good leader and leader for good. May you find success on your journey.

Remember that your position does not give you the right to command. It only lays upon you the duty of so living your life that others may receive your orders without being humiliated.
DAG HAMMARSKJÖLD *Secretary General of the United Nations (1953–1961)*

PART ONE

UNDERSTANDING LEADERSHIP

Listen to all, pluck a feather from every passing goose,
but follow no one absolutely.

CHINESE SAYING

Understanding, for most people, is the key that unlocks the door of action. You need to know about the findings of research in this field and to accept or formulate some general or integrated concept of leadership. This knowledge will then serve as a guide or sketch map as you explore further the practice of leadership later in the book.

By the time you have finished reading the sections and working on the various checklists, exercises and case studies in Part One, you should:

- know the three main approaches to leadership and be able to see how they fit together into the general theory of action-centred leadership based upon the Three Circles model.

- have become more aware of how the three areas of **task**, **team** and **individual** interact with each other, for good or ill.

- see that leadership is done on various levels, such as – in the context of organizations – **team**, **operational** and **strategic leadership**.

- and, last but not least, be confident that you are in the right field of work for you to become the best leader that it lies within you to be.

1

What you have to be

*'Reason and calm judgment, the qualities especially
belonging to a leader.'*
TACITUS

'It is a fact that some men possess an inbred superiority which
gives them a dominating influence over their contemporaries, and
marks them out unmistakably for leadership. This phenomenon is
as certain as it is mysterious. It is apparent in every association of
human beings, in every variety of circumstances and on every
plane of culture. In a school among boys, in a college among the
students, in a factory, shipyard or a mine among the workmen, as
certainly as in the Church and in the Nation, there are those who,
with an assured and unquestioned title, take the leading place, and
shape the general conduct.'

So declared Hensley Henson, Bishop of Durham, in a lecture on
leadership delivered at the University of St Andrews in Scotland in
1934. Since time immemorial people have sought to understand this
natural phenomenon of leadership. What is it that gives a person this
influence over his or her followers?

As this lecturer believed, most people thought that leadership was an 'inbred superiority' – in other words, you are either born with it or not. The born leader will emerge naturally as the leader because his qualities of mind, spirit and character give him that 'assured and unquestioned title'. Notice, incidentally, the universal unconscious assumption of the times that leadership is always a *male* prerogative.

Since 1934 quite a lot of leaders, observers of leaders, and trainers of leaders have been prepared to list the qualities which they believe constitute born leadership. The difficulty is that the lists vary considerably, even allowing for the fact that the compilers are often using rough synonyms for the same trait. They also become rather long. In fact there is a bewildering number of trait names from which the student of leadership could make up his or her portfolio. There are some 17,000 words in the English language which can be used for describing personality or character.

A study by Professor Charles Bird of the University of Minnesota in 1940 looked for 20 experimental investigations into leadership and found that only 5 per cent of the traits appear in three or more of the lists.

A questionnaire-survey of 75 top executives, carried out by the American business journal *Fortune*, listed fifteen executive qualities: judgement, initiative, integrity, foresight, energy, drive, human relations skill, decisiveness, dependability, emotional stability, fairness, ambition, dedication, objectivity and co-operation. Nearly a third of the 75 said that they thought all these qualities were indispensable. The replies showed that these personal qualities have no generally-accepted meaning. For instance, the definitions of dependability included 147 different concepts. Some executives even gave as many as eight or nine.

Apart from this apparent confusion, there is a second drawback to the qualities or traits approach. It does not form a good basis for leadership development. 'Smith is not a born leader yet', wrote one manager about his subordinate. What can the manager do about it? What can Smith do? The assumption that leaders are born and not made, favours an emphasis upon *selection* rather than *training* for leadership. It tends to favour early identification of those with the silver spoon of innate leadership in their mouths and it breeds the attitude 'You cannot teach leadership', but that assumption has now been challenged and proven to be false.

Leaders are born not made

Air Vice Marshal 'Johnnie' Johnson was the top British Fighter Command ace pilot in the Second World War. In his biography *Wing Leader* (1956) Johnson recalls his sense of loss when the legendary Group Captain Douglas Bader was shot down over France.

'At Tangmere we had simply judged Bader on his ability as a leader and a fighter pilot, and for us the high sky would never be the same again. Gone was the confident, eager, often scornful voice. Exhorting us, sometimes cursing us, but always holding us together in the fight. Gone was the greatest tactician of them all. Today marked the end of an era that was rapidly becoming a legend.

The elusive, intangible qualities of leadership can never be taught, for a man either has them or he hasn't. Bader had them in full measure and on every flight had shown us how to apply them. He had taught us the true meaning of courage, spirit, determination, guts – call it what you will. Now that he was gone, it was our task to follow his signposts which pointed the way ahead.'

It would be wrong, however, to dismiss the qualities approach altogether. It was once the custom to do so among students of the subject in the second half of the last century. For example, C.A. Gibb, an influential American psychologist and editor of *Leadership: Selected Readings* (Penguin, 1969) could conclude: 'A leader is not a person characterised by any particular and consistent set of personality traits.'

*   *   *   *   *

Incidentally, the first person to coin a list of leadership qualities in the English language was none other than William Shakespeare. The actual word *leadership* didn't exist in his day. Although it might have been among 900 new words that Shakespeare did invent, in fact it first appeared in 1822. Shakespeare does, however, refer to some generals in one of his historical plays as 'men of great leading'.

For Shakespeare, kingship and leadership are virtually two sides of the same coin. In those days, of course, a king was expected to lead his soldiers into battle from the front.

Perhaps this is a good moment to share with you a discovery that I have made recently about the origin of the verb *to lead*, a fact that has been curiously overlooked by the very large modern community of academic students and scholars of leadership.

In the several northern European languages spoken by the tribes that invaded and settled in England, the noun *led* or *læd* meant a path, track, way or course of a ship at sea. The associate verb *to lead* in turn meant simply to go or to travel. But in Anglo-Saxon or Old English, only the *causative* form of that verb survives.

In other words, uniquely for English, to lead means to *cause* others – people or animals – to go on a journey. How do you do that? Be they sheep or soldiers the principle is the same: you lead them forward from in front and they will follow you – freely, willingly, without compulsion. It is simple cause-and-effect, one known to man for 3000 years. On an ancient Sumerian clay tablet this proverb was found inscribed: *Soldiers without a king (leader) are like sheep without a shepherd.*

Shakespeare reveals a clear grasp of this principle. Contrast the armies of the two kings Macbeth and Henry V. Of Macbeth, troops on the eve of the final decisive battle compare notes and say of his commanders ruefully:

His army moves only by command,
Nothing by love.

What a difference from the army of King Henry in Agincourt, 'straining like greyhounds on the leash' to fight a French army that greatly outnumbered them. Why? Because Henry led them in front. Of course he did not make the long and inspiring speeches that Shakespeare puts in his mouth. (What he actually said on the battlefield was 'Come on fellahs!')

Not surprisingly, it is in *King Henry V* that we find Shakespeare's precious list of 12 leadership qualities, the real crown jewels:

The king-becoming graces,

As justice, verity [integrity], temperance, stableness,

Bounty [generosity], perseverance, mercy, lowliness [humility],

Devotion, patience, courage, fortitude.

Such qualities contribute to any leader's personal authority.

Notice that Shakespeare is not attempting to describe the qualities that any actual leader possesses as an individual, even King Henry. What he offers us is a list of the qualities that anyone in the role of leader – especially in the exalted office of a king (or president) – *ought* to possess. Or, if you prefer it, they are the qualities that 'become' the *role* of leader, as opposed to any given incumbent of it.

Representative qualities

When thinking about the qualities of leaders, I have found it useful to distinguish between **representative** and **generic** qualities.

By representative qualities I mean those that are required – and properly expected – in *all* members of your team. For example, all soldiers need courage, not just their commanders. Therefore it is something of a misnomer to label it a 'leadership' quality. A military leader should, of course, exemplify courage by his willingness to lead from the front where occasion demands it. Courage will not make you a military leader, but you cannot be one without it.

Generic qualities in this distinction are those which are commonly associated more specifically with leadership. They give a 'family likeness' to all effective leaders, whatever their level, field or cultural background. At the head of this chapter I give you an example: 'calm judgment'. And sketch in for you shortly the top five or six generic qualities of leadership.

You can now see why leadership often springs from having a vocation or calling. That always lies in the field of human endeavour where your talents, interests, aptitudes and general personality find their optimum use in the service of others. It is the *good* nurse or the *good* scientist, for example, who enters the frame for being considered as a leader. Thus, as a corollary, it is important to find your true vocation.

Some people have no difficulty in finding their vocation. The other day I was talking to a senior judge who told me that she knew at the age of twelve that she wanted to be a barrister. For others – and I am among their number – it may be quite some time before you find the work for which you are best suited – or it finds you.

How do you know that a person has found that natural centre? The poet W.H. Auden suggests a simple test:

You need not see what someone is doing
To know if it is his vocation.
You have only to watch his eyes:
A cook making sauce, a surgeon
Making a primary incision,
A clerk completing a bill of lading,
Wear the same rapt expression,
Forgetting themselves in a function.

Leadership, then, is really a 'second calling' – one that emerges out of one's original vocation in the fullness of time and one, incidentally, that may come to you as something of a surprise. So you do need to keep searching in the early stages of your working life until you discover what the French call your *métier* – your true profession or trade.

Some generic qualities of leadership

The French author Marcel Proust once wrote: 'The writer, in order to attain generality and, so far as literature can, reality, needs to have seen many churches in order to paint one church, and for the portrayal of a single sentiment, he requires many individuals.'

I have been lucky over a long career to meet many leaders in many different fields, and I have heard or read about a legion of other ones too. Certain personal qualities have begun to stand out in my mind as being common if not general or even universal. They are both qualities that effective leaders tend to have and qualities that – globally – people now look for in their leaders.

When the author John Buchan, then Governor-General of Canada, gave what I regard as a great lecture on the subject of leadership at the University of St. Andrews in 1930, he offered his own list of leadership qualities, but wisely added: 'We can make a list of the moral qualities of leaders but *not exhaust them*' (my italics). I agree with him. Therefore you should take the list that I offer you below as being indicative rather than exhaustive. It is open-ended. You are free to add or subtract. Here it is:

- Enthusiasm
- Integrity

- Toughness or demandingness and fairness

- Warmth and humanity

- Humility

Exercise 1: Leadership qualities

Before reading any further, take a piece of paper and write across the top the names of two individuals known to you personally and whom you regard as leaders. See if you can explore the above qualities in them by giving them a mark out of ten for each quality. Can you think of some episode where a particular quality was exemplified?

Here are a few notes on each of the generic qualities that have emerged from my own mind. Please add any additional thoughts or comments that occur to you.

Enthusiasm

Can you think of any leader worthy of the name who lacks enthusiasm? Certainly I can't. That is why it is top of my generic qualities list.

For the Greeks, enthusiasm was a divine gift. The Greek word literally means to be possessed by a god – what we would call now to be inspired. The symptoms of an enthusiastic person are well known: a lively or strong interest for a cause or activity, a great eagerness, an intense and sometimes even a passionate zeal for the work in hand. You can see why Shakespeare in *Henry IV* identifies enthusiasm as 'the very life-blood of our enterprise'. It is the life-blood of your enterprise too.

Integrity

Hard on the heels of enthusiasm comes *integrity*. I referred to it in my first lecture on leadership, 'Leadership in History', when I was in the sixth form at school and since then I have never once spoken on leadership without mentioning integrity.

Field Marshal Lord Slim once defined integrity to me as 'the quality which makes people trust you.' Mutual trust between the leader and the led is absolutely vital: lose that and you have lost everything. Moreover, it is very hard to re-establish it. As Roman historian Livy said, 'Trust being lost, all the social intercourse of men is brought to nothing.'

Integrity, from the Latin *integer*, means literally wholeness: an integer is a whole number. But with reference to people it signifies the trait that comes from a loyal adherence to values or standards *outside yourself*, especially the truth: it is a wholeness which stems from being true to truth. We know what it means when people say of a scholar or artist that he or she has integrity. They do not deceive themselves or other people. They are not manipulators. As Oliver Cromwell once wrote in a letter to a friend: 'Subtlety may deceive you, integrity never will.'

The guiding star of truth

In a letter written from New York in 1944, J.B. Yeats shared these thoughts with his son, the poet W.B. Yeats:

The real leader serves truth, not people, not his followers, and he cares little for authority or for the exercise of power, excepting so far as they help him to serve truth, and we follow him because we too, when your attention is directed to it, would also serve truth, that being a fundamental law of human nature – however unfaithful to it we may often be when misled by passion or self-interest.

Such leaders, continued Yeats, gain a ready audience:

Their command excites no anger, since we are not brought face to face with an Ego. They and all of us are serving a mistress [the truth] who really issues the orders we obey.

Just why it is that people who have integrity in this sense create trust in others I shall leave you to reflect upon at your leisure. Certainly we all know that a person who deliberately misleads us by telling lies sooner or later forfeits our trust.

There are situations in life which can test your integrity, sometimes to the uttermost. A person of integrity comes through such trials, tests and temptations. Rudyard Kipling writes of such personal moral victory in his poem *If*, which lightly sketches integrity in outline:

If you can keep your head when all about you
Are losing theirs and blaming it on you.
If you can trust yourself when all men doubt you,
But make allowance for their doubting too;

Toughness or demandingness and fairness

As a leader you need to be tough or demanding but fair. Leadership is not being popular; it is not about wanting to be liked by everyone. For leaders make demands; they set high standards; and they will not accept anything but the best. That isn't always popular.

> The great conductor Otto Klemperer expected the best from his players and didn't go into raptures when he got it. After one performance, however, he was so pleased with the orchestra that he looked at them and said, 'Good!' Overwhelmed, the musicians burst into applause. 'Not *that* good,' Klemperer said.

As Confucius commented long ago, 'The best leader is easy to serve and difficult to please.' Notice that where praise is given sparingly it is valued more. Indeed there is an Iranian proverb that says *Too much praise is worse than an insult.*

Toughness is indicative of more than being demanding in terms of the common task. Akin to resilience and firmness, it is the quality that enables you to withstand tension, strain or stress. To be firm means fixed and unshakeable, and often implies deep commitment to a moral principle. People look for this particular form of strength in a leader. As an Arab proverb puts it, 'No strength within, no respect without'. St Augustine once prayed for a 'heart of fire' for humanity's common purpose, a 'heart of love' to others, and to himself a 'heart of steel'. All true leaders have that steel in their souls.

Personally I hate war, but it is undeniable that we have learned a great deal about leadership by the experience of battle. Such crisis situations, where life and death are at stake – viewed over three thousand years and in every part of the world – are revealing about human nature, especially about what kind of leadership elicits the best response. What is evident is that soldiers respond best to leaders who are neither harsh nor soft.

The leader who liked to be liked and the commander who was not a leader

The classic description of these types of leadership comes in Xenophon's account of a military expedition of some 10,000 Greek mercenary soldiers who fought on one side in a Persian civil war and then made a famous 800 miles march through what is now Iraq and Turkey to freedom. Xenophon, who had studied leadership with Socrates and later wrote the world's first books on leadership, served on the campaign as a cavalry commander. Unsurprisingly, given the influence of Socrates as a teacher, Xenophon was an acute observer of the leadership abilities of the Greek generals.

Proxenus of the city of Boeotia was a very ambitious and well-educated young man who joined the Greek mercenary army in Persia in 40BC. He was in search of fame and fortune. Though without any practical military experience – he had been tutored by an academic in military tactics – he secured office through his political contacts as one of the expedition's six generals. Xenophon, who was invited by Proxenus to join the expedition to Persia, has left us this pen portrait of his friend and companion:

He was a good commander for people of a gentlemanly type, but he was not capable of impressing his soldiers with a feeling of respect or fear for him. Indeed he showed more diffidence in front of his soldiers than his subordinates showed in front of him, and it was obvious that he was more afraid of being unpopular with his troops than his troops were afraid of disobeying his orders.

Xenophon has also left us a pen portrait of the veteran Spartan general Clearchus. In the crisis that followed the defeat of their patrons in the battle of Cunaxa outside Babylon, when the Greeks were faced with a choice between slavery or a long hazardous march through enemy-occupied territory to the Black Sea and freedom, it was to Clearchus that everyone looked – for he had that inner steel as well as the experience of having been in such a situation before. He knew what to do. Yet Xenophon describes him as a harsh man; except when an army was in a crisis no one would voluntarily choose to serve with him. In other words, he was a commander but not a leader.

In the event, by an act of treachery, the Persians assassinated all the Greek generals and Xenophon, aged 26, was among the six elected by the soldiers to replace them. Needless to say, Xenophon aspired – not without some success – to be a great military leader.

Toughness and demandingness should always be expressed in the context of fairness: a true leader has no favourites. A former Royal Navy captain put it to me in a letter like this:

> Make demands, but not unreasonably so. Leaders need to be even-handed in their demands on subordinates. Those in the navy who demanded too much of their immediate subordinates – typically heads-of-department – generated a negative, joyless atmosphere: but those who were soft on these people would lose their community's respect. Consistency was profoundly important, not least in the handling of discipline.
>
> The Captain has to discipline proven offenders under naval law and regulation, knowing that the person (unless the offence is gross) continues as an essential working member of the warship community. Sailors understand well this need for good order: harshness will disturb them, but so will inconsistency or inappropriate leniency.

Justice or fairness is a necessary condition in all personal relations. Always honour the terms of the two-way contract that underpins any working relationship. Make sure that people are paid the correct amount and on time.

'In a personal relation between persons an impersonal element
is necessarily included and subordinated.'
JOHN MACMURRAY, *British philosopher*

Exercise 2: Have you got what it takes for a top job in leadership?

Place the following attributes in order of 'most valuable at the top level of leadership' by placing a number 1 to 25 beside them. This exercise can be done by you individually, or with others in a group.

- Ambition
- Willingness to work hard
- Enterprise
- Astuteness
- Ability to 'stick to it'
- Capacity for lucid writing
- Imagination
- Ability to spot opportunities
- Willingness to work long hours
- Curiosity
- Understanding of others
- Skill with numbers
- Capacity for abstract thought
- Integrity
- Ability to administer efficiently
- Enthusiasm
- Capacity to speak lucidly
- Single-mindedness
- Willingness to take risks
- Leadership
- Ability to take decisions
- Analytical ability
- Ability to meet unpleasant situations
- Open-mindedness
- Ability to adapt quickly to change

Now turn to page 195 and compare your answers with the ratings given to these attributes by a cross section of successful chief executives.

Warmth and Humanity

As a general principle, a 'cold fish' – meaning a totally unemotional or impassive person – does not make a good leader. For in all personal relations, be they professional or private, people do not respond well to a perceived or actual coldness in others. As the Chinese proverb says, 'You can live with cold tea and cold rice but not with cold words.'

A warmth of feeling, a general friendliness of attitude, and an unobtrusive solicitude for the welfare of individuals are all hallmarks of the good leader. Empathy is the power of entering into another's mind and imaginatively experiencing (and so fully comprehending) the way things are for that person. Empathy should lead to acts that show that you care. Caring here means taking seriously the welfare of others – your colleagues or companions in the common enterprise. Put their needs before your own.

Marcus Aurelius, Roman Emperor from AD 160 to 180, was a world leader of his day. He was burdened with a great responsibility. For much of his reign he led his legions against the Germanic tribes, who were invading the Roman Empire from the north. By nature he was a reflective thinker, a lover of practical wisdom. His *Meditations* are still a classic: a collection of aphorisms and reflections written down as much for his own guidance as a leader, as a book for others. Speaking to himself – and yet to all leaders – he writes: 'Love those people heartily that it is your fortune to be engaged with'.

Humility

In the context of leadership **humility** is best understood as the lack of arrogance. Arrogance is not an attractive attribute in anyone, let alone a leader.

Willingness to own up to one's own mistakes or errors of judgement rather than to make others into scapegoats is one hallmark of humility. Domineering, over-assertive or tyrannical men don't do that – they are always right even when their ship is sinking. Another important characteristic is open-mindedness to those views and opinions of others that challenge your own ideas or assumptions. Lastly, the ability to continue to learn, change, grow until the end of your days is the blessing that humility – not the easiest yoke – will confer on you.

Any form of play-acting or hypocrisy is incompatible with humility. That is why a humble person never pretends to be better or worse, more important or less important than they really are. As Dag Hammarskjöld wrote: 'Humility is just as much the opposite of self-abasement as it is of self-exaltation.'

*   *   *   *   *

Bear in mind also another useful distinction: between personality and character. Personality is the total impression that another person makes upon you – or you upon them. Character, by contrast, is not something which is immediately apparent or felt. Only knowing another person over time will reveal if they possess moral principles or values.

You may have noticed that we call someone's personality attractive or unattractive, but never good or bad. These moral terms we apply only to characters. And because character is essential to a true leader – more so than personality – morality is integral to leadership. Bad people may be found in leadership roles or offices, but it is an error to call them leaders.

CHECKLIST:
DO YOU HAVE SOME BASIC LEADERSHIP QUALITIES?

List the five key characteristics or personal qualities which are expected or required in workers in your field:

Now rate yourself in terms of each of them – Good, Average or Weak.

	Good	Average	Weak
_____	☐	☐	☐
_____	☐	☐	☐
_____	☐	☐	☐
_____	☐	☐	☐
_____	☐	☐	☐

	Yes	No
Have you shown yourself to be a responsible person?	☐	☐
Do you like the responsibility as well as the rewards of leadership?	☐	☐
Are you noted for your enthusiasm at work?	☐	☐
Has anyone ever used the word 'integrity' in relation to you?	☐	☐
Are you tough and demanding but fair with yourself?	☐	☐
Have you evidence to suppose that other people think of you as essentially a warm and kind person?	☐	☐
Do you balance self-confidence with humility?	☐	☐

Key points

- A leader's personality and character will breathe through all that they say and do. Who you are as a leader can be as important as what you do. *Role without personality is empty but personality without role is ineffective.*

- People expect to find in their leader a reflection of their own best qualities, especially those which characterize a *good* worker in their field. To possess these representative qualities is a necessary condition for leading others. But on top of that there are also some generic leadership qualities for you to think about.

- Good leaders *are* enthusiasts. Can you think of any true leader you have met or read about who lacks enthusiasm?

- Integrity means soundness or wholeness. A person of integrity adheres to moral principles whatever the cost. They do not lie, cheat or indulge in bribery. Integrity is the quality that makes people trust you – essential in a leader.

- Leaders need to develop some steel within themselves, for in some contexts they need to be tough and demanding but fair. *No strength within, no respect without.*

- Warmth and kindness – humanity – is a 'leader-becoming' quality.

- Humility in a leader is an antidote to pride, arrogance, self-importance and egoism.

> *I cannot hear what you are saying because what you are is shouting at me.*
> ZULU PROVERB

2

What you have to know

*'There is a small risk that leaders will be regarded with contempt
by those they lead if whatever they ask of others they show
themselves best able to perform.'*

XENOPHON

The second main approach to understanding leadership focuses upon
the **situation**. Taken to extremes, this school declares there is no such
thing as a born leader: it all depends upon the situation. Some
situations will evoke leadership from one person, others will bring it
out in another – therefore it is useless discussing leadership in general
terms.

This 'situational approach', as it is called, holds that it is always the
situation which determines who emerges as the leader and what 'style
of leadership' he or she has to adopt. Who becomes a leader of a
particular group engaging in a particular activity and what the
characteristics are in the given case, are a function of the specific
situation.

To illustrate this theory, let us imagine some survivors of a
shipwreck landing on a tropical island. The soldier in the party might

take command if natives attacked them, the builder might organize the work of erecting houses, and the farmer might direct the labour of growing food. In other words, leadership would pass from member to member according to the situation.

Note that 'situation' in this context means primarily the task of the group. If an airplane crashes in a remote jungle the person who takes command for the survival operation might not be the captain of the aircraft but the person most qualified for the job. Change the situation, and you change the leader.

The three kinds of authority at work

This 'horses for courses' approach has some obvious advantages. It emphasizes the importance of *knowledge* relevant to a specific problem situation – 'authority flows to the one who knows', as one writer put it. There are broadly three kinds of authority at work:

- the authority of **position** – office title, badges of rank, appointment
- the authority of **personality** – the natural qualities of influence
- the authority of **knowledge** – technical, professional.

Whereas leaders in the past tended to rely upon the first kind of authority – that is, they exercised mastery as the appointed boss – today leaders have to draw much more upon the second and third kinds of authority.

KENT: You have a look upon your face that I would fain call
   master.
KING LEAR: What is that?
KENT: Authority.

SHAKESPEARE, *King Lear*

But technical knowledge is not everything. It is especially important in the early stages of your career, when people tend to be specialists. As your career broadens out, however, more general skills – such as leadership, communication and decision making – come into their own. You need to acquire these general skills, for technical knowledge alone will not make you into a leader.

Michael, aged 36 years, had a brilliant career as a 'backroom-boy' in the accounts department of a British pharmaceutical company. He had passed all the examinations and specialized in tax matters, winning himself a solid reputation. He had been with the same firm for twelve years. On 'situational' grounds he should have been the ideal man to become the leader of his department when the job became vacant. When that promotion came his way, however, it took him by surprise. He was not prepared for leadership. The company was in recession; morale in the department was low. He soon found himself faced with all sorts of problems, both about the department's effectiveness and about people, where his expertise in tax law was of no help. He floundered for a while and then in desperation left the company to set up business on his own as a tax consultant.

How far are the general skills of leadership transferable from one working situation to another? The skills are certainly transferable, but often the people are not. For one reason, they do not have the sufficient technical or professional knowledge required for another field. Like courage in the case of the soldier, such knowledge and experience does not make you into a leader, but you cannot be one without it. That does not mean that leaders cannot change fields (e.g. industry for politics) as opposed to making major changes within fields (e.g. becoming managing director of an electronics company after running a car assembly plant) – but it implies that they will not be successful unless they can quickly learn the essentials or principles of the new industry or occupation.

Within a given field, such as a manufacturing industry, there are other situational determinants besides the type of produce. Size – small, medium or large – is one factor in the equation. Some industrial leaders are attracted naturally to situations where a company needs 'turning around' after a story of decline and loss of morale. Others prefer a lively, technologically advanced company going for rapid growth.

Socrates on leadership

The first person to teach what is now called the situational approach – that 'authority flows to the one who knows' – was none other than Socrates in ancient Athens. Socrates himself wrote no books but two of his students, Plato and Xenophon, published books in the form of dialogues between Socrates and various interlocutors. How far these dialogues were remembered conversations or independent creative works is sometimes hard to assess but the original inspiration of Socrates is undeniable.

In this context Xenophon and Plato, quite independently, give us the same illustrative example or parable about leadership, in both cases attributed to Socrates. The following is Plato's version.

(To understand this extract, it is useful to know that in Greek times the helmsman of a ship – the kubernator, from which our word governor comes – was also usually both the navigator and ship's captain):

> The sailors are quarrelling over control of the helm. . . They do not understand that the genuine navigator can only make himself fit to command a ship by studying the seasons of the year, sky, stars and winds, and all that belongs to his craft; and they have no idea that, along with the science of navigation, it is possible for him to gain by instruction or practice, the skill to keep control of the helm whether some like it or not.
>
> 'Have you not noticed,' Socrates asked a young man who came to him in the hope of learning how to become a leader, 'that no incompetent person ever attempts to exercise authority over our harpists, choristers and dancers, nor over wrestlers? *All who have authority over them can tell you where they learned their business.*'

Incidentally, Socrates also taught that where women know more than men (in the professional or technical sense) they will tend to be accepted as leaders. He gave the weaving industry in Athens as a good example.

The need for flexibility

Even within a given field – or within a particular organization within it – the situation varies. Some people argue that such changes require a change of leader. A company in growth may need a bustling, entrepreneurial leader; once it has established its product lines and market share that person may get frustrated and should be replaced by a different sort of person.

A chemical company on Teesside set up a new plant to make ammonia. During the commissioning phase, which lasted several years, there were many crises. The plant frequently broke down; there were accidents and all sorts of 'bugs' in the system. Eventually the plant was fully 'on stream'. In the new 'steady state' the first manager, who had thrived on the technical challenges, became inappropriate. He was replaced by a less abrasive person, who devoted far more time to developing good working relationships which is what the situation now required.

The answer, of course, is to develop as much *flexibility* as you can within your limitations. However, it is always hard to know what those limitations are. It is easy to make assumptions about them which turn out to be unfounded.

Mark never thought of himself as a leader in a crisis. He worked as a school teacher in South London. On holiday he took a party of boys and girls hill-walking in Wales. One evening, a boy who disobeyed instructions and wandered off on his own fell down a disused mineshaft. Far from panicking Mark found himself becoming calmer. He took charge of the situation.

After the rescue services arrived and had extricated the boy, they congratulated Mark on the leadership he had shown. He was completely exhausted, but he had learned an important truth about himself. Contrary to his expectations and those of his colleagues he had revealed the ability to respond to and lead in a crisis. By chance a similar but more serious accident took place in Italy that year, when a small boy got stuck down a narrow well-shaft. Complete chaos reigned. Even the President of Italy, who hastened to the scene, could not give the necessary leadership, and the child died.

Most people discover as they grow older that they are more suited by aptitudes, interests and temperament to lead in some fields rather than others. Some characteristic working situations, for example, call for speed of reaction or swift apprehension.

Some contingencies cannot be foreseen. War provides plenty of examples of such occasions when quickness of thought is essential for success. In conversation with Las Casas one day, Napoleon reflected on the rarity of this ability to react swiftly in sudden emergencies: 'As to moral courage, I have rarely met with the *two-o'clock-in-the-morning* kind: I mean unprepared courage, that which is necessary on an unexpected occasion; and which, in spite of the most unforeseen events, leaves full freedom of judgement and decision'.

No victim of false modesty, Napoleon did not hesitate to say that he was himself eminently endowed with this 'two-o'clock-in-the-morning' courage, and that he had met few persons equal to himself in this respect.

A major implication of the situational approach, as I have already suggested, is that you should select the field in which you wish to exercise leadership with care. Think of that field as being your first vocation. Usually interests, aptitude and temperament are sufficiently good guides. With my poor aptitude for music, for example, I would be wasting my time to aspire to conduct the Vienna Symphony Orchestra.

Once you have chosen your field, however, you should aim to develop maximum *flexibility* within it, so that you are the master at reading the changes in situations and responding with the appropriate leadership style. At the same time as you are growing in leadership, your technical knowledge and experience in that working field should be widening and deepening as well.

Know your field of activity

Another quality common to leaders is their willingness to work hard, to prepare themselves, to know their field of activity thoroughly. I have often heard it said of some individual: 'Oh, he'll get by on his personality.' Well, he may 'get by' for a time but if a charming personality is all he has, the day will come when he will find himself looking for a job.

I never knew President Roosevelt as well as I did some of the other world leaders, but in the few conferences I had with him I was impressed, not only by his inspirational qualities, but by his amazing grasp of the whole complex war effort. He could discuss strategy on equal terms with his generals and admirals. His knowledge of the geography of the war theatres was so encyclopaedic that the most obscure places in faraway countries were always accurately sited on his mental map. President Roosevelt possessed personality, but as his nation's leader in a global conflict, he also did his homework – thoroughly.

DWIGHT D. EISENHOWER

* * * * *

'Let each man pass his days in that wherein his skill is greatest,' wrote the Roman poet Propertius in the first century BC. As a leader, you should have the kind of temperament, personal qualities and knowledge required by the working **situation** you have chosen.

Technical competence or professional knowledge is a key strand in your authority. Yet expertise in a particular job is not enough; other more general skills are also required. These focus upon leadership, decision making and communication. These can be **transferred** as you move into a different situation in your field or change to a new sphere of work.

Within your field you should aim to widen your knowledge of the work and develop the general abilities of leading others. That will increase your **flexibility**. Even within the broad continuities of a particular industry or business *the situation will change*. Social, technical or economic developments will see to that. Are you ready?

Well, can leaders be trained?

Some will say that leaders are born, not made, and that you can't make a leader by teaching, or training. I don't agree with this entirely. While it is true that some men have within themselves the instincts and qualities of leadership in a much greater degree than others, and some men will never have the character to make leaders, I believe that leadership can be developed by training.

In the military sphere, I reckon that soldiers will be more likely to follow a leader in whose military knowledge they have confidence, rather than a man with much greater personality but with not the same obvious knowledge of his job. To the junior leader himself the mere fact of responsibility brings courage; the mere fact that by his position as the recognized head of a group of men he is responsible for their lives and comfort, gives him less time to think of his own fears and so brings him a greater degree of resolution than if he were not the leader.

I know I found this to be the case myself in 1914, when as a young lieutenant I commanded a platoon and had to lead them in charges against entrenched Germans, or undertake patrol activities in no-man's-land. By the training I had received from my superiors in peacetime, I gained confidence in my ability to deal with any situation likely to confront a young officer of my rank in war; this increased my morale and my powers of leading my platoon, and later my company.

In other words, it is almost true to say that leaders are 'made' rather than born. Many men who are not natural leaders may have some small spark of the qualities which are needed; this spark must be looked for, and then developed and brought on by training. But except in the armed forces this training is not given. In civilian circles it seems to be considered that leadership descends on men 'like dew from heaven' – it does not. There are principles of leadership just as there are principles of war, and these have to be studied.

FIELD MARSHAL LORD MONTGOMERY
An extract from a letter written to me in 1968

CHECKLIST:
ARE YOU RIGHT FOR THE SITUATION?

	Yes	No
Do you feel that your interests, aptitudes (e.g. mechanical, verbal) and temperament are suited to the field you are in?	☐	☐
Can you identify a field where you would be more likely to emerge as a leader?	☐	☐
Are you developing the authority of knowledge?	☐	☐
Have you done all you can at this stage in your career to acquire the necessary professional or specialist training available?	☐	☐
Do you have experience of more than one function in more than one field or more than one industry?	☐	☐
Do you take an interest in fields adjacent to your own and potentially relevant?	☐	☐

sometimes	☐
never	☐
always	☐

How flexible are you within your field? Are you:

Good	You have responded to situational changes with marked flexibility or approach; you read situations well, think about them and respond with the appropriate kind of leadership.	☐

Adequate	You have proved yourself in two situations, but you fear some situations; you are happiest only when the situation is normal and predictable.	☐
Weak	You are highly adapted to one particular work environment and cannot stand change. You are often called rigid or inflexible.	☐

Key points

- The authority of position remains important. But a mountaineer climbing in the Himalayas does not entrust his life to a single strand of rope. You need to weave together all three strands of authority – position, personality and knowledge – if you want to have the natural authority of a good leader.

- In order to get free and equal people to cooperate and produce great results, you need to rely upon the second and third forms of authority as well as the first.

- Authority flows *to* the one who knows. Authority flows *from* the one who knows. It is a two-way process.

- Therefore your acquisition of technical and professional knowledge is actually part of your development as a leader. You are equipping yourself with one essential ingredient.

- Leaders who share in the hardships, dangers and sufferings of their people acquire a fourth form of authority – *moral* authority. Mahatma Gandhi and Nelson Mandela are two good examples. It is a principle that applies to team leaders, too.

- People will know whether or not you have authority – you don't have to tell them, still less try to impress them with what you know. A tiger never tells you that it's a tiger.

We must have perseverance and above all confidence in ourselves.
We must believe that we are gifted for something, and that is the
thing, at whatever cost, that must be attained.

MARIE CURIE

3

What you have to do

'Not the cry but the flight of the wild duck leads the flock to fly and follow.'
CHINESE PROVERB

A third line of thinking and research about leadership focused on the group. This 'group approach' tends to see leadership in terms of functions which meet group needs: what has to be *done*. In fact, if you look closely at matters involving leadership, there are always three elements or variables:

- the **leader** – qualities of personality and character
- the **situation** – partly constant; partly varying
- the **group** – the followers: their needs and values.

The third school looked at leadership from the perspective of the group.

Group personality and group needs

Working groups are, according to my theory, more than the sum of their parts: they have a life and identity of their own. All such groups, providing they have been together for a certain amount of time, develop their own unique ethos. I call this phenomenon **group personality** – a phrase borrowed from British Prime Minister, Clement Attlee.

Group personality

It is more important that the Cabinet discussion should take place, so to speak, at a higher level than the information and opinions provided by the various departmental briefs. A collection of departmental Ministers does not make a Cabinet. A Cabinet consists only of responsible human beings. And it is their thinking and judgement in broad terms that make a Government tick, not arguments about the recommendations of civil servants. It is interesting to note that quite soon a Cabinet begins to develop a group personality. The role of the Prime Minister is to cultivate this, if it is efficient and right-minded; to do his best to modify it, if it is not.

While a collection of departmental heads mouthing their top civil servants' briefs is unsatisfactory, a collection of Ministers who are out of touch with the administration tends to be unrealistic. And a Minister who has an itch to run everybody else's department as well as, or in preference to his own, is just a nuisance. Some men will be ready to express a view about everything. They should be discouraged. If necessary, I would shut them up. Once is enough.

CLEMENT ATTLEE

In practice the phenomenon of group personality means that what works in one group may not work in its apparent twin group within the same organization.

In order for such a corporate personality to emerge, of course, a group has to be in the formative stage for some time. Then its unique character emerges. It acquires something like a collective memory. Especially when groups are in their formative stages, leaders can do a great deal to set the tone of this distinctive nature.

The other half of the theory stresses *what groups share in common* as compared to their uniqueness. They are analogous to individuals in this respect: different as we are in terms of appearance and personality, we share in common our needs – at midnight all of us usually begin to feel tired; at breakfast time we are hungry, and so on. According to my model, there are *three* areas of need present in working groups.

1 To achieve the **common task.**

2 To be held together or to **maintain itself as a cohesive unity.**

3 The **needs** which **each individual brings** with them into a group.

Task needs

One of the reasons why a group comes together is that there is a task which one person cannot do on their own. But does the group as a whole experience the need to complete the task within the natural time limits for it? A human being is not very aware of a need for food if they are already well fed, and so one would expect a group to be relatively oblivious of any sense of need if its task is being successfully performed. In this case, the only sign of a need having been met is the satisfaction or elation which overtakes the group in its moments of triumph – a happiness which as social beings we count among our deepest joys.

Before such a fulfilment, however, many groups pass through a 'black night of despair' when it may appear that the group will be compelled to disperse without achieving what it set out to do. If the members are not committed to the common goal, this will be a comparatively painless event; but if they are, the group will exhibit various degrees of anxiety and frustration. Scapegoats for the corporate failure may be chosen and punished; reorganizations might take place and new leaders emerge. Thus, adversity reveals the nature of group life more clearly than prosperity. In it we may see signs or symptoms of the need to get on effectively with whatever the group has come together to do.

Group maintenance needs

This is not easy to perceive as the task need; as with an iceberg, much of the life of any group lies below the surface. The distinction that the task need concerns things, while the group maintenance need involves people, does not help very much. Again, it is best to think of groups which are threatened – from without by forces aimed at their disintegration or from within by disruptive people or ideas. We can then see how they give priority to maintaining themselves against these external or internal pressures, sometimes showing great ingenuity in the process.

Many of the written or unwritten rules of the group are designed to promote this unity and to maintain cohesiveness at all costs. Those who rock the boat, or infringe group standards and corporate balance, may expect reactions varying from friendly indulgence to downright anger. Instinctively, a common feeling exists that 'united we stand, divided we fall', that good relationships, desirable in themselves, are also essential means towards the shared end. This need to create and promote group cohesiveness.

Lessons from wild geese

As each bird flaps its wings, it creates 'uplift' for the bird following. By flying in a V formation, the whole flock adds 71 per cent greater flying range than if the bird flew alone.

Whenever a goose falls out of the formation, it suddenly feels the drag and resistance of trying to fly alone, and quickly gets back into formation to take advantage of the 'lifting power' of the bird immediately in front.

When the lead goose gets tired, it rotates back into the formation and another goose flies at the point position.

The geese in formation honk from behind to encourage those up front to keep up their speed.

When a goose gets sick or wounded or slows down, two geese drop out of the formation and follow it to help and protect it. They stay with it until it is able to fly again or dies. Then they launch out on their own, with another formation, or catch up with the flock.

I decided to replace the term 'group maintenance' with 'team maintenance' when the time came to apply theory to training leaders. It sounded just a little less like jargon. The earliest teams in the ancient language of England were sets of draught animals pulling together. Today, of course, a 'team' is our most common word for a group of people who form a side in a game or sport. So today everyone knows what a team is. The words 'group' and 'team' are not exact synonyms; all teams are groups, but not all groups are teams.

In the context of work today, 'team' is a better word than 'group'. For the key characteristic of a team is *differentiation of roles in relation to a common goal*. The functions of the football goalkeeper, for example, differ from those of the full backs or midfield team players, yet all eleven members of the team, whatever their roles, share a common purpose and a common goal.

Individual needs

Thirdly, individuals bring into the group their own needs – not just the physical ones for food and shelter, which are largely catered for by the payment of wages these days, but also their psychological needs: recognition, a sense of doing something worthwhile; status; the deeper needs to give to and receive from other people in a working situation. These personal needs are perhaps more profound than we sometimes realize.

These needs spring from the depths of our common life as human beings. They may attract us to – or repel us from – any given group. Underlying them all is the fact that people need each other, not just to survive but to achieve and develop personality. As the African proverb says, 'It takes a whole village to grow a person'. This growth occurs in a whole range of social activities – friendship, marriage, neighbourhood – but inevitably work groups are extremely important because so many people spend so much of their waking time in them.

It is worth reflecting for a moment upon the importance of that distinction between *group* and *individual*, as opposed to allowing them to be blurred together as *people* or 'human relations' or (even worse) the 'socio-emotional area'. Of course, individuality and individualism can be taken too far. For, as indicated above, we do not become *persons* except in relation to others.

In some cultures at certain times there has been a tendency to subordinate the individual to the group. The implicit assumption when that happens is that groups are stronger, wiser and sometimes even more creative than the individuals in it. 'What the group wants' becomes the ultimate court of appeal.

Although there are cultural differences of emphasis, however, leaders should always be aware of both the **group** and each **individual**, and seek to harmonize them in the service of the third factor – the **common task**.

Understanding the individual

Individual needs are especially important in relation to motivation, which is closely connected with leadership. One of the things that leaders are supposed to do is to motivate people by a combination of rewards and threats – the carrot-and-stick approach. Yet, according to another body of theory, you and I motivate ourselves to a large extent by responding to inner needs. As a leader you must understand these needs in individuals and how they operate, so that you can work with the grain of human nature and not against it.

In this field, as in the others, it is useful for you to have a sketch map. Here, the American psychologist A.H. Maslow's concept of a 'hierarchy of needs' is still valuable. He suggested that individual needs are arranged in an order – from the stronger or more basic – we share them with animals – to the weaker but more distinctively human. These needs are often shown in a pyramid model, but actually Maslow did not present them in any visual model. Figure 3.1 is my own framework for representing them.

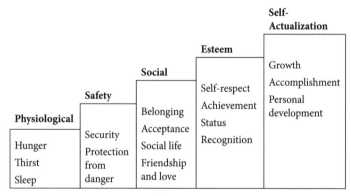

Figure 3.1

Based on Maslow's hierarchy of needs

Physiological   These are humanity's physical needs for food, shelter, warmth, sexual gratification and other bodily functions.

Safety	These include the need to feel safe from physical danger and the need for physical, mental and emotional security.
Social	This covers the need for belonging and love, the need to feel part of a group or organization; to belong to or be with someone else. Implicit in it is the need to love and be loved; to share and to be part of a family and community.
Esteem	These needs fall into two closely-related categories – self-esteem and the esteem of others. The first includes our need to respect ourselves; to feel personal worth, adequacy and competence. The second embraces our need for respect, praise, recognition and status in the eyes of others.
Self-actualization	The need to achieve as much as possible; to develop one's gifts or potential to the full in the service of others.

Maslow makes two interesting points about these needs. First, if one of our stronger needs is threatened we jump down the steps to defend it. You do not worry about status, for example, if you are starving. Therefore if you appear to threaten people's security by your proposed changes as a leader, you should expect a stoutly defended response.

Secondly, a satisfied need ceases to motivate. When one area of need is met, the person concerned becomes aware of another set of needs within him or her. These in turn now begin to motivate him. There is obviously much in this theory – when the physiological and security needs in particular have been satisfied, they do not move us so strongly. How far this principle extends up the scale is a matter for discussion.

Maslow made another significant contribution to understanding individual needs by reiterating the distinction between *instrumental* and *expressive* behaviour. Much of what we do is to meet our needs: it is a means or instrument towards an end. But a person also does or says things to express what he or she is or has become. A skater or a dancer, for instance, is expressing themselves. This perception can help us to understand why others are doing things. You could also look on leadership as both instrumental – a means of meeting task, team and individual needs – and also expressive of all that you are and can become in terms of personality, character and skill.

The Three Circles model

The next major step is to relate the three areas of need together in the Three Circles model (Figure 3.2).

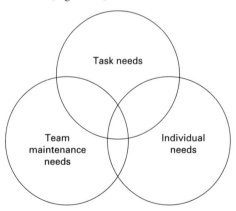

Figure 3.2

Mathematicians will recognize this framework as a Venn diagram. It was so named after the English logician John Venn (1834–1923), who first used the three circular intersecting areas to represent mathematical sets and show the relations between them.

Nowadays when I show the model on a slide or overhead, I usually colour the circles red, blue and green, for light (not pigment) refracts into these three primary colours. It is a way of suggesting that the Three Circles form a universal model. In whatever field you are, at whatever level of leadership – team leader, operational leader or strategic leader – there are three things that you should always be thinking about: *task*, *team* and *individual*. Leadership is essentially an other-centred activity – not a self-centred one.

The Three Circles model is simple but not simplistic or superficial. Keeping in mind those three primary colours, we can make an analogy with what is happening when we watch a television programme: the full-colour moving pictures are made up of dots of those three primary and (in the overlapping areas) three secondary colours. It is only when you stand well back from the complex moving and talking picture of life at work that you begin to see the underlying pattern of the Three Circles. Of course, they are not always as balanced and clear as the model suggests, but they are nonetheless there.

Many of an individual's needs – such as the need to achieve and the social need for human companionship – are met in part by participating in working groups. But an individual can also run the danger of being exploited in the interests of the task and dominated by the group in ways that trespass upon one's personal freedom and integrity.

It is a fundamental corollary of the Three Circles model that each of the circles must always be seen in relation to the other two. As a leader you need to be constantly aware of what is happening in your group in terms of the Three Circles. You can imagine one circle as a balloon getting bigger (better) and another shrinking, or you can visualize the situation as if one circle is completely eclipsed or blacked out.

Exercise 3: The Three Circles model

Cut a disc or use a round lid to cover one circle in the model. At once, segments of the other two circles are covered also. Using the disc and doing the following exercise you can begin to develop this *awareness* yourself.

1   **Cover the task circle with the disc** (Figure 3.3):

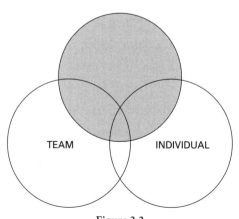

TEAM   INDIVIDUAL

Figure 3.3

If a team fails in its task, this will intensify the disintegrative tendencies present in the *group* and diminish the satisfaction of individual needs.

Polymotors, an engineering company employing 50 people, consistently failed to fill its order books after a change of management. The sales manager blamed the production head, and vice versa. They stopped talking to each other. Morale slumped. Some individuals left in disgust. Eventually the firm failed and all 50 lost their jobs in a time of high unemployment.

Can you think of another example from your experience?

2   **Cover the team circle with the disc** (Figure 3.4):

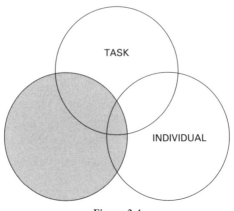

Figure 3.4

If there is a lack of unity or harmonious relationships in the team, this will affect performance on the job and also individual needs.

The Research and Development department in a large electronics firm based in Boston, USA, fell victim to group disunity. Clashes of personality and rival cliques made daily work a nightmare. Through poor internal communication the group failed to meet work deadlines. The creativity of the group dropped to zero. Absenteeism soon increased as individuals found their social needs totally frustrated at work. Eventually the department had to be divided between two others.

Can you add a further example from your experience?

3   **Cover the individual circle with the disc** (Figure 3.5):

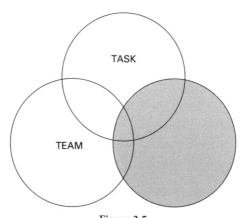

Figure 3.5

If an individual feels frustrated and unhappy, he or she will not make their maximum contribution to either the common task or the life of the team.

Henry worked in a city law office. He had been there for more than 20 years and was taken for granted. No one bothered to explain the firm's progress or prospects to him. He felt he should have been promoted some years before, but when a job became available it was given to a younger man. Henry also felt bored and frustrated because his suggestions for improving work procedures had been ignored. Gradually he withdrew into his shell. He gave the minimum effort to his work and insisted on leaving the office promptly at 5p.m. He no longer shared his lunch break with his colleagues. 'I am just waiting for retirement,' he said to me. But retirement was ten years away!

Can you think of another example?

Each individual has a piece of social power. That means that he or she can help to build up good relationships and a positive climate at work. On the other hand an individual person can, by ignorance or design, use his or her influence in a negative way. Hostile or damaging gossip behind people's backs, for example, eats away relationships in the long run as surely as acid dripping onto metal. Gossip as such is an aspect of our interest in people and human nature, and it is mostly harmless. But vicious and unfounded gossip corrodes trust at work. A positive individual may serve the group by challenging the gossipers, the harassers or the bullies. You do not have to be the leader to do that.

The circles in the model will also affect each other if there is a *positive* change in any one of them.

- Achievement in terms of a **common aim** tends to build a sense of **team identity** – the 'we-feeling', as some have called it. The moment of victory closes the psychological gaps between people: morale rises naturally.

- **Good internal communications** and a **developed team spirit** based upon past successes make a team much more likely to do well in its **task area**, and incidentally provide a more satisfactory climate for the individual.

- An **individual whose needs are recognized** and who feels that he or she can make a characteristic and worthwhile **contribution both to the task and the team** will tend to produce good fruits in both these areas.

Exercise 4: The Three Circles model

1 Can you give an example from your experience where the **team** circle has been exceptionally good – real team spirit, plenty of synergy, excellent personal relations and good communication – enabling the team to deal positively with **task** factors that would have defeated a less capable group? What have been the effects of such a group on the **individual** within it – think of a particular case known to you.

Techcom, a small firm of 150 people, had built up excellent working relations and morale was extremely high. Management and employees trusted each other and liked working together; they believed in the future of their industry and wanted to expand. Then they were hit by a downturn in the domestic market and some fierce competition from China, India and Korea. The employees volunteered to take a cut in their wages; the management promised there would be no redundancies if they could help it. Everyone redoubled their efforts. Soon business improved again and they were back in profit.

2   Add now an example where an **individual** has effectively influenced the **task** circle and also benefited the **team** as a whole.

Outstanding examples of the influence of the individual on the other two circles are often provided by two kinds of members – *leaders* and *creative thinkers*. These may be united in the same person, often called an *entrepreneur*, or they may exist separately. Certainly every team needs its creative thinkers, whether they are managers or not.

Necessary functions

In order to meet the three areas of need, as we have seen, certain **functions** have to be performed. A function may be defined as the proper or characteristic action of a person or thing. It is often one of a group of related actions, each contributing to a large action. For example, I write with a pen and in writing this sentence, both hand and eyes are fulfilling their normal and characteristic functions to contribute to a single activity. In the context of the larger activity of leading, such functions as *defining the task* and *planning* are clearly required.

Assemble a group of children in the playground with a task to perform, with or without appointing a leader, and you should be able to observe some of these functions being performed – or not performed, as the case may be.

The generic role of leader

So far we have only agreed that there are *three overlapping areas of need* present in all working groups, and that in order to meet them certain key *functions* have to be performed. The next step is the idea that these functions hang together in a set: together they form the core of **the generic role of leader**. The discovery of this generic role crowned a quest by thinkers that began long ago in ancient Athens and China, and has been pursued intently in recent times.

Expressed in its simplest form, this generic leader's role consists of (Figure 3.6):

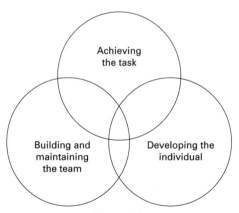

Figure 3.6

The generic role here is expressed in three very broad functions. It can then be broken down further into more specific functions, such as *planning* and *evaluating*. But you should notice that these functions – and the others explored in Part Two – are not assignable to any one circle: they have effects for good or bad on all three.

For example, *planning* looks on the surface like a task function. But there is nothing like a bad plan to disintegrate a team, lower morale and frustrate individuals. Planning hits all Three Circles: the model is a unity, or, more accurately, a diversity-in-unity.

Teams which come together to pursue a self-chosen task, such as trade unions or sports clubs, tend to *elect* their own leaders, who are responsible ultimately to the team. Where tasks are given to the team, on the other hand, the leader tends to be *appointed* by higher authority and sent to it as part of the package deal. In this case the leader is accountable first to the appointing authority and only secondly – if at all – to the team. He or she is accountable for all Three Circles.

That does not mean, of course, that the leader is going to provide all the functions needed in the three areas – there are far too many required for any one person to do that, especially in larger groups. If leaders exercise the art of leadership properly, they will generate a *sense of responsibility* in all, so that members naturally want to respond to the three sets of need. But the appointed or elected leader alone is *accountable* at the end of the day. It is the leader who should expect to be dismissed or resign if the task is not achieved, or the group disintegrates into warring factions, or the individuals lapse into sullen apathy. That is why leaders usually get paid more than the team members.

Realities of command

Almost everybody thought that it was the French general Marshal Joffre who had won the battle of the Marne in the opening year of the First World War – the crucial battle which had stemmed the advance of the German Army in front of Paris – but some refused to agree. One day a newspaper man appealed to Joffre: 'Will you tell me who did win the battle of the Marne?' 'I can't answer that,' said the Marshal. 'But I can tell you that if the battle of the Marne had been lost the blame would have been on me.'

Understanding your position as the leader in relation to the Three Circles is vitally important. You should see yourself as half-in and half-out. There should be some social distance between you and the team, but not too much. The reason for maintaining this element of distance is not to enhance your mystique, it is because you may have to take decisions or act toughly in the task area which may cause emotional reactions to be directed at you from the team and the individuals who face, in consequence, some unwelcome change. You have weakened yourself if you are on too friendly terms, or rather you have exposed yourself to pressures – 'we didn't expect that from *you*' – which you may not be able to handle.

There is a particular problem for leaders who are elected or appointed from among their colleagues and remain with the same team. To exchange the close, friendly relationship of colleagues for those of a leader and subordinates is not easy. That has been recognized for many years. When the Roman Army appointed a man to be a centurion he was always given a century of 100 men in another legion. The principle is a sound one.

You can begin to see why a degree of self-sufficiency is important for a leader. Leadership is not about popularity, as I have already said, but because leaders tend to have social, even gregarious, natures, they can find the negative reactions that come their way hard to endure. But what matters in the long run is not how many rounds of applause a leader receives but how much *respect* he or she gains, and that is never achieved by being 'soft' or 'weak' in the task, team or individual circles.

The leader's social needs can be met partly by relations with his or her team, but it is always lonely at the top. He or she can never fully share the burden with those who work for them or open their heart about their own doubts, fears and anxieties; that is best done with other leaders on their own level and preferably from outside their own organizations.

Women as leaders

Leadership is not male, military or Western. The unit in leadership is the *person*, not a man or woman. The only determinant in leadership is: who is the best *person* to fulfil the role of *leader* in this work context. One outstanding woman leader shared with me her personal philosophy of leadership – I cannot think of a better one:

My obligation as a manager is to manage in a way that enables the needs of the business to be met and the joint objectives of my colleagues and myself to be achieved. In bringing this about I have the responsibility to see that the people responsible to me who are fulfilling the task have the opportunity to extract satisfaction and fun in doing it.

Yes, I do mean fun. Difficult tasks do not preclude enjoyment and fun: when the fun goes out of a job one should seriously consider whether one is equipped to cope – being a manager today certainly requires a sense of humour.

The occasions on which I have gained most personal satisfaction from heading up a team have been when the going has been really tough and yet one is conscious of the enormous support and enthusiasm from that team of people.

I believe, however, that the effort which has to be made by every member of the team in order to achieve that unity of purpose is far greater than any demands which the task in itself could present. It is also far more rewarding. If we try to evaluate that effort against the demands of the task, it is like trying to judge whether we would have recovered from pneumonia if we had not taken the unpleasant drugs. We will never know but we are thankful to be still alive.

Creating a working environment which gives satisfaction to those operating in it is an objective in itself. This does not imply it should be an easy environment but it should be a rewarding one in terms of job satisfaction.

Leadership is a mixture of enthusiasm, striving to achieve a goal, maximizing resources and enthusing others which adds to the appeal of the successful manager.

A definition which I probably share with many other managers is what true leadership is not about – it is not about power; it is about a person's legitimate right to lead through example and self-discipline. Most of us, at least, recognise it, admire it, and respond when we see it displayed.

Remember that – contrary to what some people teach – there is no such thing as 'instant leadership'. You need to be patient with yourself, but never give up. Improvement is always possible. Like learning a new language, your conscious efforts to study and practise the principles of action-centred leadership may seem awkward and full of mistakes at first. But that is to be expected, for art lies in perfecting our natural gifts.

Eventually these efforts will drift into your subconscious mind and continue to influence your attitudes and actions without you being aware that they are doing so. And one day, people will say that you are a 'born leader'. Little do they know!

After a concert, an enthusiastic member of the audience came up to the great violinist Fritz Kreisler and said, 'I would give my life to play the violin like you did this evening.'

'I did', replied Kreisler.

CHECKLIST:
THE THREE CIRCLES MODEL

	Yes	No
Have you been able to give specific examples from your own experience on how the Three Circles or areas of need – task, group and individual – interact upon each other?	☐	☐
Can you identify your natural bias:		
You tend to put the **task** first, and are low on team and individual	☐	☐
For you the **team** seems more important; you value happy relationships more than productivity or individual job satisfaction	☐	☐

Individuals are supremely important to you; you always put the **individual** before the task or the team for that matter. You tend to over-identify with the individual	☐	☐
You can honestly say you maintain a balance, and have feedback from superiors, colleagues, and subordinates to prove it	☐	☐
Do you vary your social distance from the team according to a realistic appreciation of the factors in the situation?	☐	☐
Can you illustrate that from experience?	☐	☐

Key points

- The most useful theory about groups for the practical leader is that they are rather like individuals – all unique and yet all having things in common. What they share, according to this theory, is **needs**, just as every individual does. These needs are related to **task, team maintenance** and the **individual**. These three areas (or circles) *overlap*, for good or ill.

- Leaders in real situations are *appointed* or *elected* or they *emerge* – usually a combination of two of these methods.

- All good team members will share a sense of responsibility or 'ownership' for the three areas, but always remember that you, as the appointed or elected leader, are the only one who is accountable for all three.

- If you have a problem in one of the circles, you may well find that the cause (or causes) lies in one or both of the other circles.

- You now know the generic role of *leader* but this is the easy part! It is now up to you to think hard about what form or shape it needs to take in your own characteristic working situation.

'There is nobody who cannot improve their powers of leadership by a little thought and practice.'
FIELD MARSHAL LORD SLIM

4

Pulling the threads together

'You can be appointed a manager, but you are not a leader until your appointment is ratified in the hearts and minds of the people.'

ANON

The discovery of the generic role of leader, as outlined in this book, has proved to be incredibly useful to those who want to improve their capabilities as leaders. In the leadership field, it is a breakthrough comparable in a modest way to the discoveries of Newton or Einstein in their field of physics. Like their theoretical advances the generic role of leadership has proved to be rich in practical applications, especially the fields of leadership training.

Sharing decisions

For many the word 'leadership' implies that one person is the dictator: he or she makes all the decisions and does all the work of leadership. That is wrong. In groups of more than two or three there are too many functions required for any one person to do it all themselves. The good leader evokes or draws forth leadership from the group. He or she works as a senior partner with other members to achieve the task, build the team and meet individual needs. The ways in which this sharing takes place are so rich and varied that they cannot be prescribed. But a leader who does not capitalize on the natural response of people to the three areas hardly deserves the name.

Most practical leaders will accept that other members can help them to maintain the team or motivate and develop fellow individuals. But what about the task? And, in particular, what about *decision making and problem solving*? For these are key activities in the task area. It is useful for you as a leader to know the options open to you in decision making or problem solving.

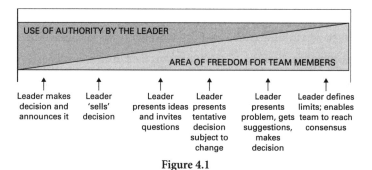

Figure 4.1

The model above (Figure 4.1) is simple: it uses the metaphor that a decision is like a cake that can be shared in different ways between the leader and the team as a whole or any individual member. At one end of the continuum the leader has virtually all the cake: he or she issues an order or command. The next point on the line is where the leader says what is to be done but gives reasons; persuades. The remaining three points on the continuum – the different shares of the cake – are fairly self-evident.

You should always bear in mind an important general principle: that the more you move to the right of the continuum or scale, the better, for *the more that people share in the decisions which affect their working life the more they are motivated to carry them out*. And as a leader you are in the business of being a motivator.

But there are factors which you should take into account in deciding where to decide. These include the **situation**, especially such variables as the time available and the complexity or specialized nature of the problem itself.

Thus, the model can help you to develop a satisfactory understanding of why leadership takes different shapes in organizations which work characteristically in *crisis* situations – those in which by definition time is in very short supply and where there is a life-or-death dimension, such as the emergency or military services, civil airlines and operating theatre teams. Here, leaders make the decisions themselves and the group is trained to respond promptly to them without argument. Research at the scenes of road accidents and forest fires confirms that people expect such firm and definite leadership from one person – they need it.

There are other such variables as the **organization** (values, tradition) and the **group** (knowledge, experience) which you should also take into account in deciding where to decide. You should always aim to be the main *consistent* as a person so that people know where they stand with you – but when it comes to decision making, infinitely *flexible*.

Developing your own style of leadership

Much argument has raged over 'styles of leadership'. In the early days, these were labelled by American theorists as 'autocratic', 'democratic' or 'laissez-faire' (or 'do-as-you-please'). That kind of simplistic thinking still lingers on.

Decision making and style should not be confused. Style implies much more than that. Nor is it possible to alter your 'style', which is an expression of yourself from situation to situation – even if you could – without running the risk of insincerity. You do not want to be a manipulator. As you will have guessed, I do not find the division into various labelled 'styles' of leadership very helpful. It does not form part of the functional leadership.

Indeed I am very wary of thinking too much about one's style as a leader at all. For I believe that style should not be something you arrive at consciously; it should come about naturally or subconsciously as you master the functions or skills of leadership.

'I should like to put on record', wrote the famous author Samuel Butler, 'that I never took the smallest pains with my style, have never thought about it, and do not know or want to know whether it is a style at all or whether it is not, as I believe and hope, just common, simple straightforwardness'. Once your personal style has developed, it will be as difficult to change as your handwriting. It will be your unique way of doing what is common – the truth of leadership, but the truth through the prism of your personality. As a Frenchman in the eighteenth century said, 'These things are external to the man; style is the person.'

Reflections of a cricket captain

Mike Brearley, one of England's most successful cricket captains, referred to my Three Circles model in his classic book *The Art of Captaincy* (Hodder & Stoughton, 1985). Here he reflects on the need to balance individual and group interest in the team. How do you build a team of individualists?

Cricket is a team game, but as such it is unusual in being made up of intensely individual duels. Personal interest may conflict with that of the team: you may feel exhausted, and yet have to bowl; you may be required to sacrifice your wicket going for quick runs. And these conflicting tensions can easily give rise to the occupational vice of cricket – selfishness.

The drive for personal success is vital to the team. Without it, a player can fail to value himself, and assume a diffidence which harms the team. He might, for example, under-rate the importance to his confidence – and thus to the team's long-term interest – of his occupying the crease for hours, however boringly, in a search for form. And I have seen a whole side in flight from selfishness, with batsmen competing to find more ridiculous ways of getting themselves out in order to prove that they weren't selfish.

It is the captain's job to coax the happy blend of self-interest and team interest from his players. Influencing the balance between individual and group. Thus he enables the group to create and sustain its identity without a deadening uniformity, and to enable the individuals to express themselves as fully as possible without damaging the interest of the whole.

Drawing upon the qualities approach

From the new perspective of the generic role, the qualities traditionally associated with leadership can be seen in a new light. They can be interpreted as helping (or hindering) the three areas of need – *achieving the task*, *building or maintaining the team*, and *developing the individual*.

First, you should apply the Three Circles to all those lists of qualities in order to pick out all the essential ones – those that can be developed. Some qualities will begin to disclose functions and specific behaviours, while some functions and outward actions will imply or express qualities. Some examples are given in Table 4.1.

Table 4.1 *Leadership characteristics*

	QUALITY	FUNCTIONAL VALUE
T A S K	Initiative	A quality which appears in many research lists. It means the aptitude for initiating or beginning action; the ability to get the group moving.
	Perseverance	The ability to endure; tenacity. Obviously functional in many situations where the group is inclined to give up or is prey to frustrations.

T **E** **A** **M**	*Integrity*	The capacity to integrate; to see the wood for the trees; to bind up parts into a working whole; the attribute that creates a group climate of trust.
	Humour	Invaluable for relieving tension in group or individual, or, for that matter, in the leader themselves. Closely related to a sense of proportion – a useful asset in anything involving people!
I **N** **D** **I** **V** **I** **D** **U** **A** **L**	*Tact*	This expresses itself in action by showing sensitive perception of what is fit, or consideration in dealing with others.
	Compassion	Individuals may develop personal problems both at home and at work. The leader can show sympathetic awareness of this distress together with a desire to alleviate it.

Some qualities are especially important because they apply to all Three Circles – *enthusiasm* is an excellent example. Not all enthusiasts are leaders, but if you have the gift of enthusiasm you almost always will spark it off in other people. It produces greater commitment to the task, creates team spirit and enthuses the individual.

Other qualities are more latent. They can be called out and express themselves in behaviour in any of the three areas. *Moral courage* and *humility*, to give two examples, are both required in certain situations. But it is important to be as specific as possible in defining when they are needed. Humility may seem an odd word because it implies to many people a cringing self-abasement quite at odds with the self-confidence, even egoism, which marks many leaders. Not so when you translate it into terms of task, team and individual.

As Aristotle taught long ago, a virtue rests somewhere between two extremes. If you use any quality to excess, or without the moderating influences of balancing qualities, it can become a liability.

Certainly too much humility – or rather humility of the counterfeit sort – is fatal to leadership, for it robs you of the proper self-confidence you should have.

Lady Violet Bonham Carter, a friend of Winston Churchill, once said to him: 'Winston, you do need to remember that you are just a worm, like the rest of us.' Churchill thought for a moment and then with a chuckle replied: 'Yes, I am a worm – but I do believe that I am a *glow worm*!'

Obviously it would take up too much time and space here to work through all the qualities most frequently mentioned with regard to leadership, seeing them as aptitudes to acquiring or providing certain functional responses – but, taking humility as an example, Table 4.1 explores the degree to which this quality is useful in the three different areas of need.

Humility in action

'A sense of humility is a quality I have observed in every leader whom I have deeply admired,' wrote Eisenhower. 'I have seen Winston Churchill with humble tears of gratitude on his cheeks as he thanked people for their help to Britain and the Allied cause'. He continued: 'My own conviction is that every leader should have enough humility to accept, publicly, the responsibility for the mistakes of the subordinates he has himself selected and, likewise, to give them credit, publicly, for

their triumphs. I am aware that some popular theories of leadership hold that the top man must always keep his "image" bright and shining. I believe, however, that in the long run fairness and honesty, and a generous attitude towards subordinates and associates, pay off.'

In a memorial speech on Eisenhower delivered to Congress in 1969, the President of the United States cited as the key to Eisenhower's character an undelivered statement prepared for broadcast over the radio in the event of the D-Day landings ending in disaster. It read as follows:

'Our landings in the Cherbourg–Havre area have failed to gain a satisfactory foothold and I have withdrawn the troops. My decision to attack at this time and place was based upon the best information available. The troops, the air force and navy, did all that bravery and devotion to duty could do. If any blame or fault attaches to the attempt it is mine alone.'

You can begin to see how the **qualities** and **functions** of leadership fit together like hand in glove. Functions are the active verbs that tell you *what* to do; qualities are the adverbs that inform *how* you do it. As the Chinese say, 'The wings carry the bird; the bird carries the wings.'

The different levels of leadership

Leadership exists on three broad levels:

Team	Leading a team or small group of about five to fifteen or sixteen people.

| **Operational** | Leading a significant part of the business with more than one team leader reporting to you. |
| **Strategic** | Leading the whole organization. |

The same generic role – symbolized by the Three Circles model – is present in each level. What differs with level is *complexity*. For example, planning is relatively simple at team level compared to the kind of strategic planning that the chief executive officer of a large organization needs to deliver.

'An institution is the lengthened shadow of one man', wrote Emerson. It used to be assumed all that was needed was a great strategic leader. This is not true. What all organizations need is excellence of leadership at *all* levels – team, operational and strategic – and good teamwork between the levels of responsibility.

Leadership and values

Is there not a difference between *good leaders* and *leaders for good*?

The original Three Circles model spoke only about needs. But it is impossible to keep values out of the picture, even if anyone wanted to do so. You have values as well as needs and they play a vital part in your decisions. Actually the relationship between values and needs is very close – we need what we value; we value what we need. But they are different. Good and bad, truth and falsehood, right and wrong, are not needs in the common sense but they do affect conduct.

You may think this is a philosophical point, not a practical one. But the best leaders have something of the philosopher in them. The fact that we are valuing humans as well as needing humans has implications which are best understood with reference again to the Three Circles model. Viewed through the prism of values, we have to search out answers to the following questions:

Task Why is this task worthwhile? What is its value to society? How is that value measured?

Group What is the commonly accepted framework of values – including ethics – that hold this group together?

Individual Do I share the same values as this group? Is the task worthwhile in my eyes?

Some people can do this kind of valuing arithmetic quite easily for themselves. But you as the leader will have to show awareness of the values of the common enterprise and interpret them for people both inside the group and outside it. Task, team and individual have to be related in values as well as in needs. That is why true leadership has an inescapable moral, or even spiritual, dimension. Without it some people may call you a *good leader* in the technical sense of the word – but you will not be a *leader for good*.

* * * * *

The Three Circles model in its active form serves as catalyst. It blends together invisibly the three main approaches to understanding leadership – qualities, situational and group or functional – into one musically integrated whole.

*A leader is the kind of person (**qualities**), with the appropriate knowledge (**situational**) who is able to provide the necessary skills (**functions**) to enable a group to achieve its task, to hold it together as a cohesive team and to motivate and develop individuals – and he or she* *does so in partnership with the right level of participation of other members of the group or organization.*

Now this cumbersome sentence is clearly not meant to stand alone as a definition. But it is a way in which I can pull together the threads for you.

CHECKLIST:
ARE YOU CLEAR ABOUT YOUR ROLE AS LEADER?

	Yes	No
Do you habitually involve your team in decisions which affect their working life?	☐	☐
More widely, do you involve team members in helping you to fulfil your generic role		
achieving the task?	☐	☐
building the team?	☐	☐
developing the individual?	☐	☐
Can you see now how qualities colour and inform functions?	☐	☐
And how performing functions with growing skill develops your qualities?	☐	☐

What 4 values does 'task' in your field honour and serve:

1 _____
2 _____
3 _____
4 _____

Do you want to be *both* a *good leader* (effective, skilful) and a *leader for good* – one who makes a positive difference to others?	☐	☐

Key points

- *A log of wood may lie in the river for years but it never becomes a crocodile*, says a trenchant African proverb. Many people are promoted to the role of team leader but they lack both leadership ability and leadership training: they become logs, not crocodiles.

- You need to fulfil – to master – the generic role. Your style, which is an expression of you, will then emerge naturally as you apply yourself to the simple functions of leadership. For leadership does consist mainly in doing some relatively simple and straightforward things, and doing them extremely well.

- Whenever possible, open the door for others in the team to have an input into decisions which affect their working lives – especially those involving significant change. They will reward you with greater commitment to outcomes.

- Leadership exists on three broad levels: team, operational and strategic. You should aim at excellence in the role of **team leader**, but also excellence as a **subordinate** to the operational leader and excellence as a colleague to your fellow team leaders and support staff.

- At whatever level of leadership you find yourself, you should think and communicate about the task in terms of values as well as needs. Then the common purpose will tend to be in harmony with the values of your team and all the individuals in the organization – including your own.

- Leadership is a form of 'truth through personality'. The truth in this case is the generic role of leader. Put that first, and only view yourself – your qualities of personality and character – in the light of that role.

Truth is ever to be found in simplicity and not in the multiplicity and confusion of things.

ISAAC NEWTON

PART TWO

DEVELOPING YOUR
LEADERSHIP SKILLS

The task of leadership is not to put greatness into humanity,

But to elicit it, for the greatness is already there.

JOHN BUCHAN

The next eight chapters focus on the main practical **functions** that you will certainly have to do or manage as a leader. They are deliberately not grouped under task, team and individual, for you should constantly remember that the circles overlap: therefore any function will affect all three.

For instance, **planning** may seem to be a task function initially, but there is nothing like a bad plan to break up group unity or frustrate the individual. The functions are the white and black keys on a piano:

they will have to be played in different sequences and combined in chords if you want to make music.

By the time you have finished reading and working on Part Two you should:

- Be able to identify clearly the main **functions** or **principles** of leadership in the three areas and have a good idea how they manifest themselves in practice.

- Know what constitutes **skill** in providing that function in certain kinds of situation.

- Be able to establish the **abilities** that you need to develop in yourself if you are going to be successful in providing those functions over a long and varied career.

5

Defining the task

'Keep the general goal in sight while tackling daily tasks.'
CHINESE PROVERB

Your primary responsibility as a leader is to ensure that your group achieves its common task. Leadership is sometimes defined as getting other people to do what *you* want to do because *they* want to do it. I do not agree. If it is *your* task, why should anyone help you to achieve it? It has to be a *common* task, one which everyone in the group can share because they see that it has value for the organization or society and – directly or indirectly – for themselves as well.

Remember that achieving the task is your principal means of developing high morale and meeting individual needs. What you do (or fail to do) in the task area is bound to affect the other two circles. So you should bear those two spheres in mind when you commit yourself and the group to task action.

As the leader, you cannot perform all the functions yourself. The group is not a flock of sheep – passive, walking lumps of mutton – with yourself as the human shepherd. They can help you and you can help them in pursuit of the common goal in various ways. The group members have energy, enthusiasm, experience, knowledge, ability or skill, and often creative ideas, to contribute to the key task functions.

Not followers but partners

The image of the shepherd-and-sheep as a leadership metaphor is very common in the ancient world. Plato used it in the *Republic*. But in a later book, *The Statesman*, he says that a leader is not at all like a shepherd because shepherds are quite different from their flocks, whereas human leaders are not very different from their followers.

Furthermore, Plato argues, people are not sheep; some are cooperative and some are very stubborn. Hence, Plato's revised view was that leaders are like weavers. Their main function is to weave together different kinds of people – such as the meek and self-controlled and the brave and impetuous – into the fabric of a society. Or, as we would say in the context of work, into an effective team.

The actual technologies involved in the task will obviously vary from group to group. But it is possible to pick out some general functions that have to be fulfilled in any working group if it is going to be successful. Inevitably without the 'clothes' of a particular business upon them, these functions will look rather naked, but they are the essential raw materials of leadership.

Be clear about your task

You may have noted already that 'task' is a fairly general word. It means a work required by an employer or a situation. Tasks come in different shapes and sizes. They are also often gift-wrapped in misleading terms. The leader, either on his or her own or with others, may have to bend their analytical powers of mind to penetrate the core of the task. One vital question is, 'How will we know when we have succeeded?' If that question cannot be answered it is usually a sign that the task is not yet clear enough.

You can visualize tasks in terms of different sizes. Personally I find it useful to distinguish between **purpose, aims** and **objectives**. Others prefer to make a rough distinction between 'short-term' and 'long-term' objectives. The dictionary will not help you here: the English language uses such words rather loosely. It is obvious, however, that there is a difference between the broader, less defined 'aim' and the more tangible or definite 'objective'.

I shall define the terms **objective, aim** and **purpose** below but, firstly, the following example may help to illustrate the differences between these types of task. It shows what is involved – and what to avoid – in communicating the objective.

Windlesham Ltd is in the business of making bath plugs. You could call that their *purpose*. They have two *aims*: to make the best bath plugs in the world and to capture 60 per cent of the world market in the next three years (they have 35 per cent at present). Jane Jackson is just one team leader at their Chobham factory. The

)

objective this week for her section is to make 30,000 one-inch plugs for a new town in Saudi Arabia.

Defining the task is not something you have to do only at the beginning of an enterprise – confusion about the end of a task can soon invade a group or organization. So you should be ready to define the end the team or any given individual is presently working towards, whenever the need arises.

Purpose   The overarching, general or integrating task of the group or organization.

Your defined purpose answers the *why* questions – 'Why are we in business?' 'Why are we doing this?' It can signify, too, the content of value or meaning in what you are doing.

Human nature craves meaning, and so if your purpose connects with personal and moral values you will not find it difficult to generate *a sense of purpose* in your team – and here *purpose* means *energy*. Your team organization will be underway, like a ship at sea.

Purpose is not the same as *vision*. A vision is a mental picture of what you want the team or the organization to look like or be in, say, three years' time.

Aims   You can break purpose down into *aims*, which are open-ended but directional. 'To become a better violinist' is an aim. You can have several – 'to improve my skills as a cook', for another example. But you shouldn't have too many, for your time and resources are limited. And that is true of teams and organizations. So once you have identified purpose choose aims carefully.

Objectives   *Objectives* are far more tangible, definite, concrete and time-bounded. The word comes from a shortening of the military phrase 'objective point'.

A familiar picture-word or metaphor for objective is *target*, originally the mark at which archers shot their arrows. A target is tangible and visible. You can clearly see the arrows sticking in the outer and inner rings of the bullseye.

A *goal* is another such picture-word. A football match takes place within clearly-defined limits of space and time; players can see instantly if they score a goal. If they are frustrated, they can go and kick the goalposts! To score goals in a match or to reach the finishing line in a marathon race calls for prolonged effort and hardship, and those overtones often colour the use of the word 'goal' in ordinary working life.

Always remember that an **objective** should be tangible, concrete, limited in time; an **aim** is less defined but is still fairly substantial rather than abstract; but a **purpose** may be couched in general or value terms.

The reason why

The apparently quite simple behaviour of a leader telling a group what to do in fact discloses several distinct levels of mental ability. These cannot be directly associated with the levels of leadership, incidentally, although there ought to be some co-relation between them. These can be identified for you, along with some common mistakes to avoid (see Figure 5.1 'Communicating the objective').

Perhaps the key one for you to focus upon first is the ability to break down the *general* into the *particular*. Aristotle taught his pupil, the future Alexander the Great, the simple lesson of how to take a general intention and turn it into a specific objective. (That is why Alexander was able to conquer the known world! Unfortunately he eventually ran out of both world and time, but that is another story.) All leaders need this skill of quarrying objectives out of aims, and then cutting *steps* into the objectives so that they can be achieved. Or, as a proverb put it more colourfully, 'If you are going to eat an elephant you have to do it one mouthful at a time'.

The reverse process – relating the *particular* to the *general* – is equally important. Leaders tend naturally to give *the reason why* something has to be done; bosses just tell you to do it. Answering the question 'why' means connecting it in the group's mind with the larger ongoing aims or purposes.

The mere presence of a sound purpose is obviously not enough. It must be *felt* to be sound by all. In other words, it must be surcharged with a strong *sense* of purpose, dynamic emotion, with a hopefulness, with an abounding, robust sense of joy in the work itself. There you will find that *making it happen* may be difficult but it will never be impossible.

CHECKLIST:
DEFINING THE TASK

		Yes	No
1.	Are you clear about the objectives of your team now and for the next few years/months, and have you agreed them with your leader?	☐	☐
2.	Do you fully understand the wider aims and purpose of the organization?	☐	☐
3.	Can you relate the objectives of your team to those larger, more general intentions?	☐	☐
4.	Does your present team objective have sufficient specificity? Is it defined in terms of time? Is it as concrete or tangible as you can make it?	☐	☐
5.	Will the team be able to know soon for itself if you succeed or fail? Does it have swift feedback of results?	☐	☐
6.	What is your team working on at present? List the 3 key success criteria that will be applied:		

_____

_____

_____

Key points

- Within the compass of the Three Circles, **defining the task** is a vital leadership function. 'Task' is a general word. It needs to be broken down into **purpose**, **aims** and **objectives**.

- *Aims* arise when *purpose* is directed and harnessed. As a leader you should be able to range up and down – using the Jacob's Ladder model (Figure 5.1) – from the particular to the general within the task circle. Such thinking is the necessary preliminary to *communication*.

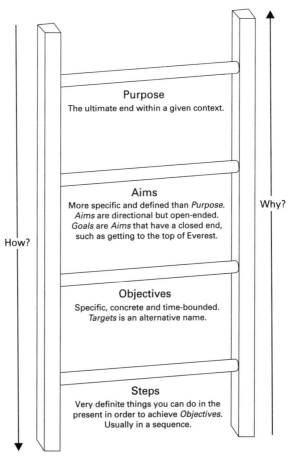

Figure 5.1 *Communicating the objective*

- Leadership implies communicating the *why* as well as the *what* and *how*, *when* and *where* and *who* of work that has to be done.

- A good leader is a forward thinker. He or she is always ready to answer the question *why*, not with a backward-looking sentence – 'because we have always done it this way' – but with a forward-looking one – 'in order to achieve this aim or that purpose'.

- Clarity about the task is often difficult to achieve. But it is essential to acquire it yourself and then to share it with others.

> *When people are of one mind and heart they*
> *can climb Mount Tai.*
>
> CHINESE PROVERB *(Mount Tai is a famous mountain in Shandong*
> *Province – the highest known to Confucius.)*

6

Planning

'Nothing is particularly hard if you divide it into small jobs.'
HENRY FORD

Planning is the activity of bridging the gap mentally from where you and the group are now to where you want to be at some future moment in terms of accomplishing a task. A plan is a method devised for making or doing something or achieving an end. It always implies mental formulation and sometimes graphic representation.

The planning function is the response to the group's needs: 'How are we going to achieve the task?' But the 'how' question soon leads you to ask also 'Who does what?' and 'When does it have to be done?' Indeed, as a planner you could do worse than memorize Rudyard Kipling's short checklist:

I keep six honest serving men
(They taught me all I knew);
Their names are *What* and *Why* and *When,*
And *How* and *Where* and *Who*

Usually, if a plan proves to be inadequate, it is because either you as the leader or the group (or both) have not pressed home these questions until you have clear and definite answers. A poor or inadequate plan means that your subsequent team action is doomed from the start. It usually turns into a drama, a comedy or tragedy, depending on the circumstances, in three Acts: Beginning, Muddle and No End. As the old adage says, 'Fail to plan and you plan to fail'.

Calmex, a major paint company, produced a new paint stripper three times faster and more effective than the other brands on the market. Helen Robinson, the marketing and public relations director, drew up an advertising plan to support the launch. But one agency failed to produce an important TV commercial on time. When Robinson remonstrated, the agency head got out the plan. 'It says here that you wanted it "as soon as possible". We thought next month would do.'

So planning is essentially about devising a method for making or doing something or achieving an end. A leader without plans is not likely to be effective. So, how do you develop skill as a planner?

Searching for alternatives

There is a skill in conjuring out from your own mind and from the group a sufficient number of alternative methods to choose from.

Shortage of time obviously can limit you. If you are trying to avoid a car crash, you do not have time to consider all the feasible alternatives: you have to select the first one that flashes into your mind. Therefore one of the first questions you should ask is, 'How much time have I got?'

If necessary, test those time constraints to see if they are *real* as opposed to *assumed* ones. We often have more time to make a plan than we think we do. Provided there is not a crisis or an emergency and you know how much time is available, you can apply yourself to using that planning time to good effect. Keep a careful check on the time, however, because it soon goes.

Another factor you must take into account is the resources available to you in identifying the different feasible courses of action or solutions. What *people* can you consult? You may have noticed how good leaders lead when faced with a significant difficulty – whether an operational challenge or some crisis.

They hold in check their own hunches or intuitions as to what should be done. Establishing the facts is their absolute priority, coupled with identifying the salient factors, the ones relevant to the decision that needs to be made. Then, when discussing the options that arise from the realities of the situation, the leader tends not to declare their own thoughts prematurely.

A trained instinct causes the effective leader always to listen first to the ideas, courses of action or solutions proposed by the team. If time allows, he or she asks those junior to speak before their seniors. The leader then summarizes what has been put forward, decides on the way forward, and explains the logic behind it. Such an approach can be deeply satisfying to all participants and is likely to yield the best solution.

Table 6.1 summarizes the different levels of group participation in decision making, showing under what circumstances these are useful or appropriate.

The team or individuals who are going to carry out the plan are especially important in the decision-making process. Remember that fundamental principle: *the more that people share in the decisions which affect their working life, the more they are motivated to carry them out.* Think out the appropriate strategy for involving them on the lines of an appreciation of the three degrees of participation described in Table 6.1.

Table 6.1 *Sharing decisions*

Degree of participation	Useful	Not useful
1 You present a tentative plan subject to change if another in the group comes up with a better one.	When group time is short. Where you have much experience in the field and are fairly sure you are right.	Where time is plentiful and the group is as technically competent as you are. When you are only going through the motions, being unwilling to accept any changes.
2 You present the problem and get suggestions from the group	It involves the group much more than 1. Groups can be far more creative than their individual members – including you. ('Two heads are better than one.')	Can be time consuming. If the group lacks sufficient knowledge and interest in the matter in hand.
3 You present a firm plan, subject to only minor changes of detail to improve it.	When you are absolutely sure that you are right. Where time is critically short.	Where the group needs to be more involved in the thinking and deciding if it is to be really committed to action.

In the positions shown in Table 6.1 (which you may take up in different situations during a single working day), it is assumed that you as the leader will take the decision to do it *this* way rather than *that* way at the end of the first phase of planning. Should you ever allow the group as a whole to take the decision? That depends upon what might be called the 'political constitution' – written or unwritten – of the group or organization, which usually makes these things fairly clear. Some main types of situation can be identified as shown in Table 6.2.

Table 6.2

Position	Notes
You are an **elected** leader, leading the group who elected you.	The group as a whole may well wish to choose between alternative outline plans itself. It may expect you to put the matter to a vote or to test for consensus.
You are an **emergent** leader, without any formal authority at all. The group look to you for a lead.	You can influence the group to adopt one course rather than another. But, if you want to stay leader, you'll have to go along with the group choice if it contradicts your own judgement. The political constitution will be informal and often vague. Both you and the group may appeal to precedents in decision making.
You are an **appointed** leader, with a clearly defined authority.	If you are ultimately accountable for the work of the group, you can justly claim to have the last word on the decision.

As you will see, there are some 'grey areas' in sharing decision making with a group. You may be two, if not all three, of these types of leader. The political leader in many democratic countries where there is a constitutional monarchy or equivalent presidency, for example, is emergent, elected and appointed. Even if you have the authority to propose your own plan and carry it out, or arbitrarily to choose, among the several possibilities put forward, the one that you like best personally, you may be reluctant to use that authority, for you want to involve and commit the group. But keep a firm control of the process.

In groups where all members are roughly equal in competence the choice between alternatives may be debated hotly. Leaders as well as members need to be able to put the case for a course of action as persuasively as they can, while remaining open-minded and honest enough to recognize the truth when it emerges from any quarter. Such a process belongs to the essence of democracy. 'Whenever people can be persuaded rather than ordered – when they can be made to feel that they have participated in developing the plan – they approach their tasks with understanding and enthusiasm', said Eisenhower. He recalled that Churchill was a persuader during the planning phase:

Indeed his skill in the use of words and logic was so great that on several occasions when he and I disagreed on some important matter – even when I was convinced of the correctness of my own view and when responsibility was clearly mine – I had a very hard time withstanding his arguments. More than once he forced me to re-examine my own premises, to convince myself again that I was right – or accept his solution. Yet if the decision went against him, he accepted it with good grace, and did everything in his power to support it with proper action. Leadership by persuasion and the wholehearted acceptance of a contrary decision are both fundamentals of democracy.

It becomes clear that without leadership, any form of democracy can be inert and feeble.

As the Chinese saying goes, 'A thousand workers, a thousand plans'. To get anything agreed and done calls for leadership. When all people can feel themselves to be equal in value, if not in knowledge and experience, that is the beginning of true leadership – not its end. As

Montesquieu wrote, 'To suggest where you cannot compel, to guide where you cannot demand, that is the supreme form of skill'.

How to be more creative

Planning doesn't sound very creative, does it? All those typed schedules and drawings or diagrams. But a plan grows from an idea. That idea is the germ of a method, solution or course. Perhaps the most common mistake is to make an *unconscious assumption* which limits the number or kind of methods. 'It is quite clear', a director of human resources announced to her colleagues recently, 'that we can do only two things about Bill Jackson in accounts: move him sideways or make him redundant. Which will it be?'

The better leaders have always resisted this binary thinking – black or white, this or that. But many managers (and academics) do think in terms of either/or, because it offers a spurious clarity. This is an important stage in some cases (e.g. a judge summing up for a jury) to reduce the judgment to an issue (either this or that) if it can be done. But it is fatal to do it too quickly, so that you totally ignore the third, fourth or fifth possibilities, which might have included the best suggestions. So you should make sure that you or your group generate enough options. As Bismarck used to say to his generals, 'If you think the enemy has only two courses open to him you can be sure that he will choose the third!'

Alfred P Sloan, the great President of General Motors in the United States, is reported to have said at a meeting of one of his top committees 'Gentlemen, I take it we are all in complete agreement on the decision here.' Everyone around the table nodded assent. 'Then', continued Sloan, 'I propose we postpone further discussion of this matter until our next meeting to give ourselves time to develop disagreement and perhaps gain some understanding of what the decision is all about.'

In most situations, the three or four feasible alternatives can be identified by straightforward observation, thought, and group discussion. But there is often a 'creative solution', so called because it is hidden until someone actually discovers it. ('How obvious and simple. Why didn't we think of that?') If the two puzzles in the following exercise are not already familiar to you, they will make the point.

Exercise 5: Creative solutions

1   Connect up the nine dots with four consecutive straight lines, i.e. without taking your pencil off the paper.

        O   O   O
        O   O   O
        O   O   O

2   Take six matchsticks and put them on a table in front of you. Now arrange them into a pattern of four equilateral (equal sided) triangles, without breaking the matches. There are at least two acceptable solutions.

Now turn to page 196 for the answers.

Karl Dunckner, the psychologist who invented the matchsticks problem in the 1920s, made the point that we develop *functional*

fixedness as we grow older. So, for example, we view a hammer as
only for knocking in nails. The first step towards greater creativity
is to try to free ourselves from such assumptions, useful though
they are in everyday life.

Exercise 6: Functional flexibility

List twenty-five uses for a hammer other than knocking in nails or
wrenching them out. You have five minutes.

You may find it hard to think of new ideas or to generate them
from other people if you have picked up the habit of instant criticism.

Negative criticism directed at your own ideas or someone else's
will destroy them. The technique known as 'brainstorming' works
by encouraging people deliberately to *suspend judgement* – to refrain
from criticism and to produce as many ideas as possible. On the other
hand, if you want to stifle creative thinking here are some useful
phrases for you:

'That will never work.'
'Don't waste my time with such rubbish.'
'We have tried it before.'
'If you thought it up it must be wrong.'

The concept of group climate is important here. Some groups
are like a white frost on an April morning in England: they kill off
the blossoms of ideas which might one day fruit into plans. The
atmosphere is negative, hypercritical and anxious. Other groups are
like warm mornings in May: positive, encouraging and confident.

Leadership is a key factor in turning a negative group into a positive one. One important skill is asking leading questions, as shown with Table 6.3, Some skills in generating ideas.

Each of us has some ten thousand million brain cells and they are probably the most expensive resource your organization hires. In order to secure the best quality plan you will need to involve the team's brain cells as well as your own. It pays off a high dividend in commitment.

Quality Circles originated in Japan and there were 20 Circles in 1961, by 1980 a staggering 10 million workers were members of Circles. Little wonder then that Japan had seized world leadership in quality by the end of the 1980s, especially in the production of motor vehicles and electrical goods. Who would then have thought in 1945 that one day Toyota and Honda would challenge Ford and General Motors for dominance in their own home American market?

The general principle behind Quality Circles is simple. A team meets for about one hour every week in company time to discuss work problems, investigate their causes and recommend solutions. These solutions are then implemented directly or presented to management for agreement on action.

Table 6.3 *Some skills in generating ideas*

Questions/Statements	Notes
Bringing in 'Bob, you have had experience in several other industries, how did they tackle this problem?'	Meets individual needs as well as the task.

Stimulating	
'Imagine we were starting from scratch again. How would we do it?'	Brains are like car engines. They need warming up by outrageous ideas or thought provoking suggestions.
Building on	
'Can't we develop the idea behind Mary's suggestion of cutting down the number of files? How else can we improve our information storage system?'	Entails seeing the positive idea or principle in a suggestion and taking it further.
Spreading	
'We can also include Jim's suggestion about time-keeping and Mary's point about safety in the plan.'	Helps to develop a team solution. A creative process of weaving separate threads and loose ends together into a whole.
Accepting while rejecting	
'Mike's proposal is an interesting and helpful one, but it would take us rather too long so we must leave it on one side for the present.'	You are accepting Mike, but rejecting his plan in a gracious way. He will not be resentful, and may come up with the winning idea next time.

When Fort Dunlop in the UK was taken over by Sumitomo, the Japanese management asked for money-saving ideas from the workforce. A junior employee saved the company £100,000 a year in electricity payments by suggesting that every other fluorescent light in the huge factory did not need to be used – an idea that he had had for years!

Making a contingency plan

Constructing a work programme and a time plan follows naturally from the choice of a method to achieve the task. Depending on the technology involved, that work programme can vary enormously in size and complexity. The only general guidance that can be given is to keep it *as simple as possible*. But there is one aspect of planning which experienced leaders tend to devote more attention to than others – contingency planning.

No one can ever make a perfect plan. You cannot foresee every eventuality. Once thinking stops and committee action begins – the real 'point-of-no-return' in decision making – there are bound to be some contingencies – things that happen by chance or through unforeseen causes which affect what you are doing.

A good plan will make some provision for the contingent in human affairs. A prudent householder usually keeps a bit of money in reserve in case some of the things that are liable to happen actually do so. A wise general also keeps a reserve corps available in case the enemy does something he had not expected. So you should build a certain amount of flexibility into your plan so that you are not caught out by unforeseen (but not improbable) happenings.

To repeat the point, a good leader thinks ahead. He or she uses their imagination in a disciplined way to picture those contingencies. Their imagination is like a mental radar screen. Once a possible contingency has been picked up they must estimate the chances of it occurring and make provision accordingly. Thus, you have to become an educated guesser. 'All the business of war, and indeed all the business of life,' said the Duke of Wellington to a friend over dinner one evening, 'is to endeavour to find out what you don't know by what you do. That's what I called guessing what was at the other side of the hill.' In the language of leadership qualities it is known as *foresight* – seeing what others cannot see because they are not tall enough to look over the hill.

*   *   *   *   *

Thus, as a planner, you should be developing the necessary abilities for **sharing decision making** where feasible, as well as **creative imagination** and **foresight**. To these should be added, of course, the necessary professional knowledge and technical skills required in your particular work.

CHECKLIST:
PLANNING YOUR WORK

	Yes	No
Have you listened to specialist advice before making your plan?	☐	☐
Did you consider all the feasible courses of action and weigh them up in terms of resources needed/available and outcomes?	☐	☐
Have you a programme now which will achieve your objective?	☐	☐
Is there a provision for contingencies?	☐	☐
Did you and the team actively search for a more creative solution as the basis for your plan?	☐	☐
Have you made the plan as simple and as foolproof as possible, rather than complicated?	☐	☐
Does the plan include any necessary preparation or training of the team or individuals?	☐	☐
Are you aware of your PNR (Point of No Return), the point at which no changes can be made without causing unacceptable confusion?	☐	☐
Do you keep the plan under regular review?	☐	☐

Key points

- **Planning** is a key activity in any working group or organization, and it constitutes one of the foundation principles of leadership. Like all the other functions, it can be done with skill and effectively – or poorly and ineffectively.

- Once the task has been defined, the first step in planning is to search for alternatives. More often than not this work is best done in consultation with others. It is important to not only remain open to, but indeed to actively encourage, new ideas or possibilities.

- You should aim to become a **creative thinker** yourself and learn how to stimulate creative or innovative ideas in the group and in each individual.

- No plan, however original, is perfect. Indeed, experience tends to teach us that any plan – even if it is a good one – will have a tendency to go off the rails. It is certainly not wise to plan projects on 'best case' scenarios. There should be tolerances or fall-back strategies.

- Glitches – unexpected problems or malfunctions – will occur. So the leader with practical wisdom acts in the knowledge *that there are a number of things that can go wrong.* Not all of these possibilities can be foreseen. Always plan for foreseeable contingencies.

- If you are flexible you can adjust to your plan any new factors in the situation as they arise. As a French general once said to me, 'A plan is a very good basis for changing your mind'.

Adventure is just bad planning

ROALD AMUNDSEN, *Arctic explorer, first man to reach the North Pole*

7

Briefing

'To know how to do it is simple, the difficulty is doing it.'

CHINESE PROVERB

The pilots and aircrew shuffle in their chairs and talk among themselves. Outside the rain beats down on the large Nissen hut that serves as a conference room. At 10.00 hours promptly the adjutant calls the room to attention and General Savage strides in and takes his position in the centre of the low platform, feet apart and facing the audience. 'There will be a practice mission this morning. That's right – practice. Our strike photographs show that we haven't been hitting the target lately.'

This is a scene from the Second World War film *Twelve O'Clock High* (1949), which starred Gregory Peck, about the first meeting of the 918 Bomb Group called by their new commanding officer. It is a film I know exceptionally well as it served as a case study in the original two-day functional leadership or action-centred leadership courses that I pioneered. It still remains the feature film that best illustrates the nature and practice of leadership, especially in the military context.

Such briefing sessions are held in all kinds of other organizations, albeit without the drama of a wartime situation. In them the leader is performing a basic leadership function – *briefing the team*. He or she is informing or instructing them thoroughly in advance – in advance, that is, of the action required of them.

And, by wider extension, *briefing* in this context covers all the situations where you are addressing either the team or an individual member in your role as leader. So it can be sometimes quite informal and conversational.

The *content* of a team briefing meeting in the formal sense – gathered together – is the result of carrying out two previous functions: defining the task and planning. After stating the objectives and why they are important, you have to describe the plan – in outline first and then in greater detail (although this second activity can be delegated to a subordinate or colleague, as General Savage does in the film). It is essential for you to answer the question which will be in everyone's minds, 'What is my part going to be?' So ask yourself before and after such a briefing meeting questions such as:

- Does everyone know exactly what his or her job is?
- Has each member of the group clearly defined targets and performance standards agreed between them and me?

The main purpose of a briefing meeting is to allocate tasks to groups and individuals, to distribute resources and to set or check standards of performance. Each person should know at the end what is expected of them and how the contribution of their sub-group or their own efforts will fit in with the purposeful work of everyone else.

Again, just to emphasize the point, *briefing* in this wider sense is an on-going function. You don't do it just once at the beginning of a project and then forget about it.

Effective speaking

A consideration of the leader's method brings us to your need to develop your communication skills. Here, the specific ability to speak effectively to your team and to other groups is going to be important for your progress. How do you do it?

To begin with the good news: you do not have to become a great orator. You should not concern yourself with the tricks of rhetoric, the techniques taught to would-be demagogues in ancient Athens. The only test is whether or not you can speak in such a way that you *move the group to the desired action*. Demosthenes said to a rival orator: 'You make the audience say, "How well he speaks!" I make them say, "Let us march against Philip!"'

Seven tips for becoming a good speaker

1 Examine the true purpose of each communication. Always ask yourself what you really want to accomplish with your message.

2 Be mindful, while you communicate, of the overtones as well as the basic content of your message.

3 When it comes to content, bear in mind the enduring value of truth in any human communication. As one Ethiopian proverb says: *Over truth there is light.*

4   Consider the total physical and human setting whenever you communicate. Check your sense of *timing* against the situation. There is a time and a place for everything.

5   Take the opportunity, when it arises, to convey something of help or value to the receiver.

6   Be sure that your actions support your communication. Words should interpret what is done and action should accompany words. Eventually our words should become acts and our acts our truest words.

7   Seek not only to be understood but also to understand – be a good listener.

An element of persuasion, in the sense of explaining why in a convincing way, will enter into most briefing or communicating meetings. But it will happen more naturally if you have mastered the skills of speaking or briefing. We can identify five sets of skills involved in communicating effectively with action in mind. These skills are set out in Table 7.1, together with some examples of how to do it.

Be clear

Clarity is the cardinal principle of power or effectiveness in both speech and writing. Therefore good communication begins in the mind. The poet Nicolas Boileau expressed this truth in 1674:

What is conceived well is expressed clearly,
And words to say it will arise with ease.

Clear thinking issues in a clear utterance: if your thoughts or ideas are a bit confused, vague or fuzzy, then they will be that much less easily understood or perceived.

Thus the application of this principle begins a long way back from the boardroom or executive office, in the struggle to achieve clarity in the uncertain weather of the mind. This entails mastering the intellectual skills of analysing, synthesizing and valuing. You can find out more about these in my companion book, *Effective Decision Making*.

However, it should not be supposed that what is *clear* is automatically *true*. Someone once said that George Bernard Shaw's head contained a confusion of clear ideas. Be that as it may, truth does not always come purified and translucent, and 'All that glitters is not gold'.

Clarity is a mercenary value: it serves well whoever is prepared to pay the price for it. That price includes the willingness to suffer muddle, confusion and ambiguity before the clouds part, the dust settles, and the issue, problem or course of action becomes crystal clear. If it becomes a matter of communicating to others, the combination of truth and clarity is extremely irresistible, certainly so in the long run.

My first masterclass

One of the masters of our time in applying the principle of Be Clear was Field Marshal Montgomery. His wartime briefings became a legend to those who heard him.

As a boy at St Paul's School I heard ex-pupil Lord Montgomery speak when he visited his old school to describe his D-Day plans. He spoke in the very building that was used during the Second World War as Allied Headquarters – indeed, in the same lecture room he and the other generals had used for their final presentations to King George VI and Churchill. So, it was not difficult for myself, a sixteen-year-old boy, to capture the 'atmosphere', as Montgomery liked to call it.

Above all, his refreshing clarity lingers. Brigadier Essame emphasized it in the following account of Montgomery at work in Ronald Lewin's *Montgomery as a Military Commander* (1971).

He could describe a complex situation with amazing lucidity and sum up a long exercise without the use of a single note. He looked straight into the eyes of the audience when he spoke. He had a remarkable flair for picking out the essence of a problem, and for indicating its solution with startling clarity. It was almost impossible to misunderstand his meaning, however unpalatable it might be.

Briefing and group work

Briefing sessions or conferences – work meetings – allow you to do some valuable work in all Three Circles models, making general points connected with the specific matter in hand. In the task area, for example, you can make it the occasion (as General Savage did) for taking charge. A certain amount of assertiveness is often required of leaders and the group will accept it – even welcome it – if the situation calls for it. You can stress the *team* approach to the task in hand, thus building up team spirit. You can meet *individual* needs by listening to and acknowledging the help of those who help you to achieve the ends of the meeting. It can also be an opportunity for emphasizing the significance of each individual's contribution to the success of the enterprise.

General Savage in the film was using the medium of the briefing meeting – called for the purpose of informing and instructing – to convey or share his vision, standards or values.

Table 7.1 *Briefing skills*

Skill	Definition	How you can do it
Preparing	The ability to think ahead and plan your communication.	Give a beginning, middle and end in your talk. Prepare good visual aids, not too many. Arrange the room in advance.
Clarifying	The ability to be clear and understandable.	Unravel the difficulties in your own mind first. Avoid obscure ways of putting things. Seek clarifying questions.
Simplifying	The ability to render complex matters into their simple forms.	Relating the unfamiliar to the familiar with homely analogies. Avoid complicated terminology. Give an overview or outline first. Summarize.
Vivifying	The ability to make a subject come alive.	Use of vivid language or methods, even gimmicks. Be enthusiastic and aim to enthuse the group. Use humour if possible.
Being yourself	The ability to cope with nerves and to behave naturally in front of an audience.	Breathe deeply. Eliminate nervous habits. Bear yourself well.

A short course on leadership

The six most important words: 'I admit I made a mistake.'
The five most important words: 'I am proud of you.'
The four most important words: 'What is your opinion?'
The three most important words: 'If you please.'
The two most important words: 'Thank you.'
The one most important word: 'We.'
And the least most important word: 'I.'

*   *   *   *   *

Perhaps the word most closely associated with leadership in people's minds is **communication**. A good leader communicates. But it is important for you to become more specific than that. In this chapter, we have looked at the *briefing* function. That apparently simple activity does call for a number of skills that can be developed.

At the first level of leadership you should strive to become competent at briefing your group on objectives and plans. At the more senior level, one day you may have to brief the organization, a much more demanding task.

At all levels there are individuals who need to be briefed in clear and simple language. Such occasions – team, organizational or individual – are not to be seen merely in terms of the task. They are also opportunities for you to create the right **atmosphere**, to promote **teamwork**, and to get to know, encourage and motivate each **individual** person.

CHECKLIST:
BRIEFING

	Yes	No

Do you regularly brief your team on the organization's ☐ ☐
current plans and future developments?

How would you rate yourself on each of the five skills of briefing
effectively:

	Good	Adequate	Weak
Preparing	☐	☐	☐
Clarifying	☐	☐	☐
Simplifying	☐	☐	☐
Vivifying	☐	☐	☐
Being yourself	☐	☐	☐

In what specific ways can you improve your skills?
1.
2.
3.

	Yes	No

Can you identify the most effective briefing talk by   Yes   No
a team leader that you have ever heard? In one   ☐   ☐
sentence, why was it effective?

                                                         Yes   No

Could your organization improve its two-way   ☐   ☐
communication of information and instructions with
those responsible for carrying them out? If so, how?

Has more than one person described the way you speak to the
team as:

CLEAR ☐   SIMPLE ☐   CONCISE ☐

                                                         Yes   No

Are you known as a leader who listens?   ☐   ☐

Key points

- Your first aim as a leader is to make the task truly common by communicating or sharing it – that is, assuming that you have been given a definite objective by your superior which the group does not know about. But that is only one type of situation, a relatively straightforward one. *Briefing* – two-way communication – runs through all your work as a leader.

- You don't have to be an orator! The hallmark of your talking as a leader is that you should be CLEAR. And you won't be clear in speech if you are not clear in your mind.

- Life and work are complex. Your job as a leader is to make the complex SIMPLE enough so that effective action can be taken. Don't, however, be over-simple or simplistic. But don't, on the other hand, go out of your way to make it complicated.

- A silent, inarticulate or even laconic leader is a contradiction in terms. You cannot perform any leadership function without instrumental words. But don't be long-winded! Don't get to like the sound of your own voice! Be CONCISE.

- All communication is two-way, because as persons we are reciprocal. You may never become a great speaker but you can become a great listener. The world needs listening leaders.

Speak properly, and in as few words as you can,
but always plainly; for the end of speech is not ostentation,
but to be understood.

WILLIAM PENN, *founder of Pennsylvania*

8

Controlling

Between the idea

And the reality

Between the motion

And the act

Falls the Shadow

T S ELIOT, The Hollow Men (1925)

Making it happen is central to effective leadership. It is not enough to define your objective or make a workable plan. All too often a shadow falls between the intention or plan, and what actually happens – or doesn't happen, as the case may be.

As a leader you are there to see that it happens. Once work has started you have to oversee it so that it reaches a successful conclusion. That calls for the skills which I have roughly grouped under the function of *controlling*. (The British Army calls it *executing*.)

'No one will miss this bag of gold if I slip it under the table. In the account I'll put it down as travel expenses.' In the Middle Ages the royal servants in the various departments of State were not above helping themselves from the till. Therefore it was necessary to supervise their accounts of payments and receipts by keeping a duplicate roll. Then you could check or verify payments *contra rotulus*, against that (second) roll.

A contraction of this Medieval Latin phrase has given us our modern word *control*. In its wider sense, 'controlling' means checking and directing action once work has started to implement the plan. And in this context the primary function of controlling also includes co-ordinating team efforts and **harmonizing** relations as work proceeds.

At the outset you have to establish that you are in charge. Then you have to maintain that control. Again, that does not mean that you will do all the leadership work yourself. But in their eagerness to help there is always a danger that a sub-group or an individual member will in effect take over control from you. Such specialists or strong individuals can be given their head on occasion, but you should keep the reins firmly in your own hands. However quiet you may be by nature, you must not allow anyone to dominate you or the group. Brave self-assertion is needed. Timidity is out. It is fatal to authority if you give instructions (as orders, suggestions or questions) and act like a small boy who throws a stone and runs away.

Once work has started on a project it is vitally important that you *control* and *coordinate* what is being done, so that everyone's energy is turning wheels and making things happen – or most of the group's energy anyway, for human beings are as inefficient as old steam engines and steam is always escaping one way or another. But *most* of that synergy or common energy of the group should be fully deployed in implementing the common plan and producing the desired results.

A sense of partnership

'I made the soldiers partners with me in the battle. I always told them what I was going to do, and what I wanted them to do. I think the soldiers felt that they mattered, that they belonged.'

FIELD MARSHAL MONTGOMERY

How do you do it? The secret of controlling is to have a clear idea in your mind what should be happening, when it should occur, who should be doing it and how it should be done. The more effectively you have involved the group in your planning the more likely it is that they too will have a similar clear picture of what is required. The ideal is that the team or the individual with whom you are dealing should become self-controlling, so as to regulate his/her own performance against standards or the clock. 'We have only got two hours left, and so we shall have to work harder to get the job done to meet the deadline.' Your aim as a leader is to intervene as little as possible.

> A leader is best
> When people barely know that he exists.
> Not so good when people obey and acclaim him,
> Worst when they despise him.
> 'Fail to honour people,
> They fail to honour you';
> But of a good leader, who talks little
> When the task is done, the aim fulfilled,
> They will all say, 'We did this ourselves.'

LAO-TZU, 6th Century BC

Your object, then, in directing, regulating and restraining is to ensure that the group's work keeps within bounds or remains on course like a ship at sea. That is the sole criterion of your effectiveness as a controller. You have oversight, which means you should be able to look at the whole picture. If obstacles or difficulties crop up in the path of the adopted course, you are then in a good position to help the group to cope with them.

The stance of a controller is to be where the action is, but observing rather than doing. If you watch a good leader in the execution phase of an exercise or project, his or her eyes are never still. The pattern of ability here is: **look, think,** and **intervene** only where strictly necessary and with the minimum exercise of power.

Obviously if a safety standard is being ignored and someone is in danger of losing life or limb, your thought processes will be instant. But much of what you pick up on will be below standard or performance (especially if you are inclined to be a perfectionist) and you will have to make a judgement whether or not to intervene immediately or to make the points later.

Making it happen

In the Second World War the leader of Britain, Winston Churchill, was constantly stimulating his colleagues to greater efforts, as well as the nation by his inspiring speeches. Nobody who worked near him or within his reach had an easy time.

'I am certainly not one of those who need to be prodded,' he said. 'In fact, if anything, I am the prod.'

If you decide on intervention, the principle is to use the minimum force possible. If you imagine that you are at the controls of an ocean racing yacht, you do not normally have to force the rudder about or lunge around at the crew with a boathook. In order to get the group on to its agreed course again you may only have to touch the controls – a quiet word or even a look can do the trick. As the Arabs say, 'Who does not understand a look cannot understand long explanations'. The personal course you have to steer as a leader should take you between the two black rocks of *too much interference* and *lack of direction*. Many a leader is shipwrecked in these foaming straits.

The leader as first companion

John Hunt, now Lord Hunt, led the British expedition that first climbed Everest in 1953. These words are from a talk he gave in 1959, entitled 'Leadership in the Modern Age'.

'Firstly, I will give you my definition of leadership, as applied to someone to whom other people are entrusted. To me, it is best described as the art of inspiring others to give of their best, and the courage to use this art. That is what leadership means to me: it demands that the leader operates from inside his group, not from above it; that in setting a good example, he does not steal the initiative of the others; in other words that he takes his full share – but no more than his share – of the job in hand. This implies a willingness not merely to decentralize, or apportion the burden, but an ability to persuade each other member of the group that his is an equally essential job, and that each has his own liberty as well as responsibility to develop that part as a whole.

'Good leadership derives from a right attitude to the job of leading; that this is only one of the jobs to be done. A leader has been well described as a "first companion". Then, of course, it is the art of blending the efforts of everyone concerned to produce a combined result.'

If the plan is going well and the group is composed of self-disciplining people, you can sometimes have time to help an individual or a sub-group with their part of the task. If you want everyone to work hard you must not give the impression that you are standing around with nothing to do. Yet you should always remain in such a position that you can instantly take control if things begin to go wrong.

Some leaders make the mistake of getting so involved in a piece of work that they forget their responsibility for the whole. You do not see the whole forest if you are busy cutting down a tree – which your woodman could do better than you if only he could get his hands on *his* axe! Setting an example of hard work is always a good idea, as long as it does not detract from your function as director and controller.

Controlling a meeting

Taking the chair in committees and at meetings is a leadership role. Therefore the model of the Three Circles applies. Decision making is essential too, because that is usually what meetings and committees are about. Consequently there is relatively little to be added specifically about the chairperson's job providing you have grasped the elements of good leadership. What matters most then is to observe and learn from experienced chairpersons at work. They are rare people, and you should not miss the opportunity of watching closely how they conduct a meeting so that the tasks are achieved, the group works as a team and each individual contributes effectively according to their talents.

There are some leadership functions needed more frequently in committees and meetings than elsewhere. The skill of silencing people in a firm but friendly way has to be developed. The skill of testing for consensus is also vital. A good chairperson will sense that area of consensus, which is rather like the invisible ever-moving centre of a shoal of fish. Here his or her ability to read non-verbal behaviour – a raised eyebrow, a half-smile, a vigorous nod – can be significant. If you watch a good leader in the chair you will notice that he or she always keeps an eye upon the faces of the committee members. Lastly, the skill of summarizing may have to be employed more than once during a meeting. It is a means of taking bearings, to ensure that the ship is still on course.

True consensus is not always possible, even if it is normally desirable, because it can be very time consuming. It occurs when communication has been sufficiently open for all to feel they have had a fair chance to influence the decision and the 'feeling of the meeting' emerges without voting.

True consensus

When alternatives have been debated thoroughly by the group and everyone is prepared to accept that in the circumstances one

particular solution is the best way forward, even though it might not be *every* person's preferred solution.

The most important test is that everyone is prepared to act as though it was their preferred solution.

Self-control

If you cannot control yourself you are unlikely to be able to control others. Take bad temper as an example. An occasional explosion of anger does no harm if the provocation is evident and treatable. Leaders tend not to be placid, and the capacity for justified anger is important. Your people should be wary of getting on the wrong side of you by being wilfully inefficient or ineffective. But bad temper is a very different matter. It is far from being a harmless weakness, a mere matter of temperament. If you are easily ruffled, quick-tempered or 'touchy' by disposition, people will diagnose it as caused by a lack of patience, kindness, courtesy or unselfishness.

Remember, however, that all your weaknesses are merely tendencies to act in a certain way. They do not guarantee that you will do so. Hundreds of leaders have successfully curbed their fiery tempers, harnessing the energy released rather than allowing themselves to simply 'blow their top'. 'Leaders,' said Paul of Tarsus, 'should not be "easily provoked".'

There are plenty of other aspects in us that invite self-control. Just controlling your tongue – that unruly member – can be a formidable job. The encouraging fact is that each small victory over one of these tendencies makes the next encounter a little easier. As Shakespeare wrote in *Hamlet*:

Refrain tonight,
And that shall lend a kind of easiness
To the next abstinence, the next more easy;
For use almost can change the stamp of nature.

Calm, cool and collected

There are some situations which naturally invite fear or anxiety. Everyone must be aware that fear is contagious. An animal can smell or sense whether or not you are afraid of it, so can people. You only have to recollect how panic can suddenly seize a crowd without a word being spoken. But courage – the resource in us which enables us to contain or overcome fear – is also contagious.

Being human you will have as much fear and anxiety as anyone else in the group or organization. But fear paralyses. If you want the group to continue working then fear has to be neutralized. If you can calm yourself, remaining a still centre in the storm, that calmness will be radiated to others. 'If you can keep your head when those about you are losing theirs and blaming it on you,' as Kipling wrote. If you can do that, then people will calm down and begin to think and work constructively.

Sometimes a calm leader's appearance on the scene can change the situation. In his novel *Typhoon*, Joseph Conrad graphically describes the relief of a first mate in a severe gale: 'Jukes was uncritically glad to have his captain at hand. It relieved him as though that man had, by simply coming on deck, taken at once most of the gale's weight upon his shoulders. Such is the prestige, the privilege, and the burden of command.' Compare the Arab proverb: 'A frightened captain makes a frightened crew.'

In his Cabinet room when he was Prime Minister of the United Kingdom, Harold Macmillan kept a card in front of him with this sentence in his own handwriting: 'Quiet, calm deliberation disentangles every knot.' That is a good practical rule of thumb for a leader to follow.

Military history gives us some vivid examples of great leadership in this respect. I think of General Robert E. Lee at Gettysburg when he knew the battle was lost. As one officer beside him in that dark hour wrote: 'His face did not show the slightest disappointment, care or annoyance, and he addressed to every soldier he met a few words of encouragement. "All will come right in the end, we'll talk it over afterwards." And to a Brigade Commander speaking angrily of the heavy losses of his men: "Never mind, General, all this has been my fault. It is I who have lost this fight, and you must help me out of it the best way you can".'

My own favourite example comes from Napoleon's disastrous Russian campaign. On the retreat from Moscow in that terrible winter of 1812, the Emperor entrusted the command of the rear-guard – the most hazardous post of all – to Marshal Ney. At one point the rear-guard found itself under constant attack by the Russian forces. They sustained heavy losses; they were starving, short of ammunition and freezing in the bitter cold. According to Ney's aide-de-camp, Colonel de Fezensac, their position seemed utterly hopeless.

But the presence of Marshal Ney was enough to reassure us. Without knowing what he intended or what he could do, we knew that he would do something. His confidence in himself was equal to his courage. The greater the danger the more prompt was his resolution, and once he had decided on what course to take he never doubted of success. Thus, even at a moment like this, his face showed no sign of indecision or anxiety. Everyone turned his eyes to him, but no one ventured to question him. At last, seeing one of his staff near him, the Marshal said in a low voice:

'It is not well with us'.

'What are you going to do?' replied the officer.

'Get to the other side of the Dnieper'.

'Where is the way to it?'

'We shall find out'.

'But what if it is not frozen over?'

'It will be'.

When they reached the Dnieper, the French soldiers managed to get across the frozen river but the ice was not thick enough to bear the weight of their train of cannons. One of Ney's staff officers fell through the ice and Ney himself crawled on his hands and knees to haul him out. In the language of this book, despite the immense burden of his responsibilities for *task* and *team*, Ney found time for the need of an *individual*. When Napoleon later heard of Ney's exploits in the retreat from Moscow he commented, 'Ney is the bravest of the brave'.

CHECKLIST:
CONTROLLING

	Yes	No
Do you maintain a balance between controlling with too tight a rein and giving the group too much freedom to do as it pleases?	☐	☐
Are you able to coordinate work in progress, bringing all the several parts into a common, harmonious action in proper relation with each other?	☐	☐
On those occasions when you are directly involved with the 'technical' work, do you make arrangements so that the team requirements and the specific needs of its members are not ignored or overlooked?	☐	☐

What were the three characteristics of the most effective chairperson of meetings you have come across?

1. ....

2. ....

3. ....

When you are 'in the chair' do meetings run over the time allotted for them?

Never ☐   Sometimes ☐   Always ☐

Is the organization you work for noted with customers on account of its control systems in the following areas:

Quality of product/service	☐
Delivery	☐
Keeping costs down	☐
Safety	☐

	Yes	No
Above all, do you have a reputation for being a 'doer', a leader who makes things happen in spite of difficulties?	☐	☐

Key points

- The function of **controlling** involves checking against standards and directing the course of work in progress to a successful conclusion. **Co-ordinating** and **harmonizing** implies that you as leader are watching the team at work, poised to intervene constructively if the need arises, and ensuring that the team is working as a team at its best.

- That does not mean you should have no work of your own or never lend a hand. But primarily your responsibility for the whole team effort should come first. If you have performed the foregoing functions well and trained your team, it should become largely **self-controlling**.

- Meetings in particular call for skilled control by the chairperson. Remember that the Three Circles model applies to all work meetings – so put it into practice.

- The power of your physical presence is especially important when things are either going wrong or when there is a danger of that happening and it is all falling apart. At such times what is needed is a positive climate. Your spirit – your calmness – will communicate itself to the group. You can inspire confidence. Make your decision and brief the group on what is to be done. Remember that in such crisis situations almost any decision is better than none.

- Remember, in the words of an Irish proverb: *There is no strength until there is co-operation.*

- It is useless to seek to control others if you cannot control yourself. 'In managing human affairs,' said Lao-Tzu, 'there is no better rule than self-restraint.' That implies not only such things as controlling your use of time but also managing your emotions so that they do not take control of you. Fear or anxiety, anger or impatience: these are your unruly lodgers that you should keep under lock and key.

There must be a beginning of any great matter, but the continuing unto the end until it be thoroughly finished yields the true glory.

SIR FRANCIS DRAKE

9

Motivating

'If you know the nature of water it is easier to row a boat.'
CHINESE PROVERB

As a leader you have to be able to get the group and its individual members moving – or keep them moving – in the desired direction. This general ability to move and excite people to action is now called *motivation*. The subjects of your motivating activity will be the team and the individual. By extension, especially if or when you become a strategic leader, it will come to include the *organization* as well.

Various theories of motivation, based largely on the contributions of Maslow, began to influence industry and management in the late 1950s. In *The Human Side of Enterprise* (1960) Douglas McGregor classically pointed out that managers often operated under one of two sets of contrasting explicit or implicit assumptions about people, which he labelled Theory X and Theory Y. These are outlined in Table 9.1.

McGregor made the point that what we believe about a person can help that person to behave in that way (the 'self-fulfilling prophecy'). If you tell someone you believe that they are bone idle, for example, they will tend to live up to your prediction. If you have a high regard for them, although that is not strictly justified by the facts, they may well rise to meet your expectations.

Table 9.1 *Assumptions about man*

Theory X	Theory Y
Man dislikes work and will avoid it if he can.	Work is necessary to man's psychological growth.
	Man wants to be interested in his work and, under the right conditions, he can enjoy it.
Man must be forced or bribed to make the right effort.	Man will direct himself towards an accepted target.
Man would rather be directed than accept responsibility, which he avoids.	Man will seek, and accept, responsibility under the right conditions.
	The discipline a man imposes on himself is more effective, and can be more severe, than any imposed on him.
Man is motivated mainly by money. Man is motivated by anxiety about his security.	Under the right conditions man is motivated by the desire to realize his own potential.
Most people have little creativity – except when it comes to getting round management rules!	Creativity and ingenuity are widely distributed and grossly underused.

Natural leaders have always acted on that assumption. They hold a creative or strategic belief in people, despite evidence to the contrary. 'Trust men and they will be true to you,' said Emerson. 'Treat them greatly and they will show themselves great.'

The *Pygmalion* effect

In George Bernard Shaw's *Pygmalion*, Eliza Doolittle explains:

'You see, really and truly, apart from the things anyone can pick up (the dressing and the proper way of speaking and so on), the difference between a lady and a flower girl is not how she behaves, but how she's treated. I shall always be a flower girl to Professor Higgins, because he always treats me as a flower girl, and always will, but I know I can be a lady to you, because you always treat me as a lady, and always will.'

Pygmalion was a sculptor in Greek mythology who carved a statue of a beautiful woman that subsequently was brought to life. George Bernard Shaw's play, *Pygmalion* (the basis for the musical hit, *My Fair Lady*), has a somewhat similar theme; the essence is that one person, by his effort and will, can transform another person. And in the world of management, many executives play Pygmalion-like roles in developing able subordinates and in stimulating their performance. What is the secret of their success? How are they different from managers who fail to develop people?

Another expression of this understanding of man as essentially self-motivating appeared in the work of Frederick Herzberg, another American, who involved himself far more than Maslow in industry. Like Maslow's thought, Herzberg's contribution was a significant one to our understanding of leadership.

In the mid-1950s Herzberg and his associates interviewed 203 engineers and accountants in Pittsburgh to find out why they found some events in their working lives highly satisfying and others highly dissatisfying. Herzberg separated the factors involved into two factors,

which he called 'motivators' and 'hygiene' factors. The motivators –
outlined in Table 9.2 – provided longer-lasting satisfaction to
individuals. The hygiene factors, which he listed as including company
policy and administration, supervision, interpersonal relations, salary,
status, job security, personal life and working conditions, cause us
dissatisfaction if they are wrong. But if you give a person more of a
hygiene factor you will only either reduce their dissatisfaction or else
give them a short-lived sense of satisfaction.

Table 9.2 *Herzberg's two-factor theory*

What motivates or satisfies people at work is not the opposite of what
demotivates or dissatisfies them. There are two separate sets of factors at
work. This list describes those identified by Herzberg as motivators.

Factor	Definition
Achievement	Sense of bringing something to a successful conclusion, completing a job, solving a problem, making a successful sale. The sense of achievement is in proportion to the size of the challenge.
Recognition	Acknowledgement of a person's contribution; appreciation of work by company or colleagues; rewards for merit.
Job interest	Intrinsic appeal of job; variety rather than repetition; job holds interest and is not monotonous or boring.
Responsibility	Being allowed to use discretion at work; shown trust by company; having authority to make decisions; accountable for the work of others.
Advancement	Promotion in status or job, or the prospect of it.

Although Herzberg, you will have noticed, included 'supervision' in
his set of hygiene factors – those which cause great dissatisfaction
when they are not met or are 'wrong' – he was clearly mistaken on this
point. Leadership, a word incidentally that Herzberg never used, is

more than just part of someone's job context: in many instances it is
integral to the job itself. You only have to look at the list above to see
that leaders can play a large part in the 'motivating' factors.

The 50–50 rule and the eight principles of motivating

I came to the conclusion that Maslow, Herzberg and that school of
thought are only half-right about motivation. *Fifty per cent of our*
motivation comes from within us as we respond to our internal
programme of needs; fifty per cent comes from outside ourselves,
especially from the leadership we encounter in life.

   This 50–50 rule is not meant to be mathematically accurate; rather,
it is indicative of the ever-shifting balance between internal and
external influences. From it I have deduced eight principles for leaders
who want to motivate others. These are as follows.

Be motivated yourself

As a leader you need to be enthusiastic. You can't light a fire with a
dead match! There is nothing as contagious as enthusiasm. Certainly,
great designs are not accomplished without enthusiasm. As the
Bedouin proverb puts it: 'What comes from your heart is greater than
what comes from your hand alone.'

Select people who are highly motivated

It is hard to motivate people who are not motivated already. Therefore
look for people who have the seeds of high motivation in them. As

Oliver Cromwell once said: 'Give me the red coated captain who knows what he is fighting for and loves what he knows.' Build your team not from those who talk enthusiastic but from those who show eagerness for the business in hand and steady commitment in their actions.

As an old folk saying has it: 'Don't beat the pig to try to make it sing. It wears you out and annoys the pig. Much better to sell the pig for bacon and buy a canary.'

Treat each person as an individual

Theories and principles apply to the generality of people. You will never know how they apply – even if they apply – to any given individual person unless you observe them and talk to them. You will learn what motivates them, and perhaps also how their pattern of motivation has changed over their lifetime.

The Greek dramatist Menander once said: ' "Know thyself" is a good saying, but not in all situations. In many it is better to say, "Know others".' As a leader you should aspire to know others. A good shepherd knows his sheep by name. John Steinbeck put it thus: 'No one really knows about other human beings. The best you can do is to suppose that others are like yourself.'

Set realistic and challenging targets

The best people like to be stretched – they welcome feasible but demanding tasks. Don't make life too easy for them! Fortunately, business life provides a series of challenges, enough to keep everyone on their toes. Without toil, trouble, difficulty and struggle there is no sense of achievement. Your skill as a leader is to set and agree goals, objectives or targets that both achieve the task and develop the team and its individual members.

Remember that progress motivates

We all need positive feedback that we are moving in the right direction, for that encourages us to persevere in the face of difficulties. 'I will go anywhere, as long as it is forwards,' said David Livingstone to a friend. If you as leader can show to your team – and to each individual member – that progress *is* being made, that in itself will feed their determination to press forward on the path of success.

Create a motivating environment

Leadership calls for social creativity every bit as important and demanding as the artistic creativity of painter, sculptor or composer. You are there to build teamwork, and that is a creative activity. More widely, all leaders in an organization should work together to ensure that it is an interesting, stimulating and challenging place of work.

Remember the 50–50 principle: about half of our motivation comes from outside ourselves, especially the people around us. Their commitment, passion and stimulating creative minds can awaken the sleeping powers within us. Your job as a leader is to foster that learning and motivating environment.

Provide fair rewards

We have a built-in sense of fairness. It is sometimes not easy to ensure equity in salary and bonuses, but it is important to remember that the perception of unfair rewards does have a demotivating effect on most people – Herzberg was right in that respect. As a general principle, financial (and other) rewards should match the relative value of contribution, according to the market assessment for any particular kind of work.

Give recognition

At best, money is a crude measure of the value of work. Is a pop star really worth a thousand times more money than a brain surgeon? A good leader should be swift to show recognition to *all* members of the team or organization, however indirect their contribution is to the overall task. You should work on the principle of 'credit where credit is due'. Where the work of people is valued there is always motivation to do it – and to do it well.

Motivation and inspiration

If you apply the eight principles described above, you will find that in the course of time you tend to become an inspiring leader. For you will be already going far beyond trying to move people by financial incentives or appeals to fear, those levers which the old-style bosses of yesteryear used to the exclusion of all else. You will be imparting to others your own spirit. Admiral Lord St Vincent once wrote in a letter to his young Captain Nelson: 'I never saw a man in our profession who possessed the magic art of infusing the same spirit into others which inspired their own actions as you do. All agree there is but one Nelson'. Through the ages the true leaders have had that same capacity to inspire willing effort in others.

Leaders who inspire

Xenophon knew from personal experience what it was like to inspire soldiers on campaign, but he was also the first and greatest student of leadership. Here is his composite portrait of the inspiring military leader.

'For some commanders make their men unwilling to work and take risks, disinclined and unwilling to obey, except under compulsion, and actually proud of defying their commander. Yes, and these commanders cause these men to have no sense of dishonour when something disgraceful happens.

Contrast the brave and skilful general with a natural gift for leadership. Let him take over command of these same troops, or of others if you like. What effect has he on them? They are ashamed to do a disgraceful act, think it better to obey and take pride in obedience, working cheerfully – each man and all together – when it is necessary to work.

Just as a love of work may spring up in the mind of a private soldier here and there, so a whole army under the influence of a good leader is inspired by love of work and ambition to distinguish itself under the commander's eye. If this is the feeling of the rank and file for their commander, then he is an excellent leader.

So leadership is not a matter of being best with bow and javelin, nor riding the best horse and being foremost in danger, nor being the most knowledgeable about cavalry tactics. It is being able to make his soldiers feel that they must follow him through fire and in any adventure.

So, too, in private industries the man in authority – the director or manager – who can make the workers eager, industrious and persevering – he is the man who grows the business in a profitable way.

On a warship, when out on the high seas and the rowers must toil all day to reach port, some rowing-masters can say and do the right thing to raise the men's spirits and make them work with a will. Other rowing-masters are so lacking in this ability that it takes them twice the time to finish the same voyage. Here they land bathed in sweat, with mutual congratulations, master and oarsmen. There they arrive with dry skin; they hate their master and he hates them.'

Quite how an effective leader so inspires a group of people – even the lowest class of citizens in ancient Athens who manned the oars in their naval galleys – so they become a willing and even enthusiastic team will always be a little mysterious. But it can be done – *you* can do it. And when people are truly inspired material rewards become irrelevant and the fear of punishment is totally absent. *You do not need a whip to urge on an obedient horse,* the Russian proverb says.

*   *   *   *   *

The proverbial wisdom of the nations has a wealth of advice – some of it contradictory – for leaders on the subject of giving praise and blame. Situations and the individual personalities of those concerned must guide you on which proverb to follow but the range of proverbs is thought-provoking. They reveal to us just how important giving and receiving praise is within the fabric of social life – someone once said to me that **praise was the oxygen of the human spirit**. But it is difficult both to give and to receive it well.

Praise and blame: some proverbs

An honest man is hurt by praise unjustly bestowed

Too much praise is a burden

I praise loudly, I blame softly

Our praises are our wages

The most pleasing of all sounds – that of your own praise

Be sparing in praise and more so in blaming

Praise a fool and you water his folly

Praise is always pleasant

Praise makes good men better and bad men worse

Finally, goodness in the moral sense is the sure foundation of leadership. Honesty, integrity, moral courage, justice or fairness, all make for better, more effective teams. Virtues such as these in leader and member alike mean that the energies of the team are being spent on the task, not on infighting, politicking, back-stabbing, intriguing and mutual suspicion. As with most things, it is up to you as a leader to set the example.

CHECKLIST:
MOTIVATING

	Yes	No
Have you agreed with your team members their main targets and continuing responsibilities, together with standards of performance, so that you can both recognize achievement?	☐	☐
Do you recognise the contribution of each member of the team and encourage other team members to do the same?	☐	☐
In the event of success, do you acknowledge it and build on it? In the event of setbacks, do you identify what went well and give constructive guidance for improving future performance?	☐	☐
Can you delegate more? Can you give more discretion over decisions and more accountability to a sub-group or individual?	☐	☐
Do you show to those that work with you that you trust them by, for example, not hedging them around with unnecessary controls?	☐	☐
Are there adequate opportunities for training and (where necessary) re-training?	☐	☐
Do you encourage each individual to develop his or her capacities to the full?	☐	☐
Is the overall performance of each individual regularly reviewed in face-to-face discussion?	☐	☐
Does financial reward match contribution?	☐	☐

Do you make sufficient time to talk and listen, so ☐ ☐
that you understand the unique (and changing)
profile of needs and wants in each person,
enabling you to work with the grain of nature
rather than against it?

Do you encourage able people with the prospect ☐ ☐
of promotion within the organization, or – if that
is impossible – counsel them to look elsewhere
for the next position fitting their merit?

Can you think of a manager who delegates ☐ ☐
(a) more effectively (b) less effectively than you
do? What are the results in each case?

(a) ☐

(b) ☐

Key points

- Human motives have their sources in the deeper needs and values within people. A need that becomes conscious is called a want. A leader can sometimes help the process by which needs are transformed into wants.

- To provide the right climate and opportunities for these needs to be met for each individual in the group is possibly the most difficult and certainly the most challenging and rewarding of the leader's tasks.

- People are indeed self-motivating, but we all respond well to positive influence in the form of **encouragement** from others. To *encourage* means to give hope, confidence or spirit – and sometimes to give active help as well.

- Fifty per cent of our motivation comes from within us, and fifty per cent from outside, especially from good leadership. Therefore, as a leader make sure that you get your fifty per cent right by practising these principles:

  - Be motivated yourself

  - Select people who are highly motivated

  - Treat each person as an individual

  - Set realistic and challenging targets

  - Remember that progress motivates

  - Create a motivating environment

  - Provide fair rewards

  - Give recognition.

- As a leader you should always be ready to support, moderate or encourage your team or the individual during the course of a day. In the Zulu language there is a name *abakhwezeli* – it means literally 'the one who keeps the fire going'. It is not a bad definition of the motivating function of a leader.

- No description of human nature can ever be complete, but you only have to be 90 per cent right about 90 per cent of the people with whom you are dealing. Of course there will be bad days. Of course there will be exceptions. But people respond to those who have vision. That vision should include a realistic but uplifting view of people, such as the one I have sketched above.

If you treat people as they are, they will stay as they are.
But if you treat them as they ought to be, they will become
bigger and better persons.

GOETHE

10

Organizing

'The summits of the various kinds of business are, like the tops of mountains, much more alike than the parts below – the bare principles are much the same; it is only the rich variegated details of the lower strata that so contrast with one another. But it needs travelling to know that the summits are the same. Those who live on one mountain believe that their mountain is wholly unlike all others.'

WALTER BAGEHOT

Just as there are leaders who prove to be extremely weak as organizers, especially when they are unwisely promoted into their 'level of incompetence' in the organization, so there are some who have a talent for organizing but lack ability in the other major functions. Assuming that you already have the potential for being a good organizer and some experience in organizations, the aim of this chapter is to sharpen your skills.

Organizing is the function of arranging or forming into a coherent unity or functional whole. It can mean systematic planning as well, but that is a function we have already covered. Here, organizing means more the kind of structuring that has to be done if people are to work as a unit with each element performing its proper part. It is essentially concerned with getting right the relation of the whole and the parts. It is a manifestation of perhaps a deep vocational impulse to impose or bring order in place of chaos. Order is the value that lies behind society, just as freedom is the value that lies behind the individual. A balance needs to be struck in any team or organization between order (the whole) and freedom (the individual).

Organizing your team

In order to achieve anything you may have to give your group some structure, especially if it is large (more than 5–10 people) and the task is complex. These structures may be temporary – for the duration of the exercise – or permanent.

If the group in question is a permanent or continuing one, with individuals joining and leaving it, it may well be part of a larger organization. In which case the organization as a whole, or your predecessor as leader, may already have sub-groups with leaders. You may wish to maintain that ready-made structure, or introduce changes. The essence of organizing at this level is to break up the group as it gets larger into smaller sub-groups and to appoint leaders who are responsible to you.

This will give you a second communications system. The first is the method of talking to the whole group yourself and listening to what they say – two-way, face-to-face communication. The content of these team meetings will include *purpose*, *policies*, *progress* and *people*. The advantage of this method is that it is not liable to the communication failures which occur when you are passing messages to another person via a third (and fourth and fifth . . .) party. But it is time consuming.

Much – but not all – of this communication work can be delegated to sub-leaders. A good and well trained sub-leader will not only pass on and interpret messages accurately, but will also report back to you clearly and concisely the reactions, constructive ideas or suggestions which arose in his or her sub-group meeting on such areas as:

- How to do the *task* more effectively.
- How we can work better as a *team*.
- How *individuals* can make their optimal contribution.

The structure not only gives you a second communication system, it also provides you with another option in your decision making and problem solving strategy. You can now put a problem to, or ask for proposed courses of action or solutions from, your inner leadership team of sub-group leaders rather than to the group as a whole. In choosing when to use each of these two methods for decision making, it is important to be flexible according to the needs of the situation, the size and character of the group and the kind of decision involved.

If your group is a very large one (20 or more) it is essential to sub-divide it and appoint (or allow the members to elect) leaders responsible to you, otherwise the individual needs described elsewhere in this book are not going to be met. You want each of your sub-leaders to involve their people in the task, develop a team approach and to inspire, encourage and control individuals as necessary. The more the sub-groups can take on these functions themselves, with the minimum of supervision, the better. But that, paradoxically, requires good leadership from you and their sub-group leader.

Providing you take the Three Circles model as your guide you can undertake this structural survey without too much difficulty, especially if you set up a small but representative steering group to work with you. The key is to ask yourselves the right questions. Some suggestions are outlined in Figure 10.1.

Whether you start at the top and work downwards, or vice versa, it is important to be systematic about it. You are trying to see how the pieces of the jigsaw fit together.

At the first-line level you should need an answer to the question 'How large or small should the primary group or groups be in this industry?' A good guideline is to establish how many people one team leader can 'do the Three Circles' with – if you catch my meaning.

The Roman Army, like the Greeks before them, operated with a primary group of ten soldiers led by a *decanus*. In large Benedictine

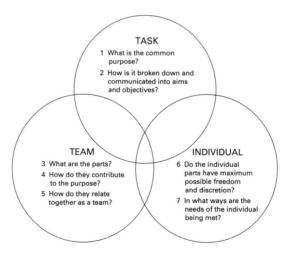

Figure 10.1

monasteries, the leader at the strategic level was the Abbot, and the 'operational leaders' were the heads of the major departments. For the 'team leaders' – those responsible for ten monks – St Benedict in his *Rule* borrowed the title *decanus*. It is the origin of the academic and church title *dean*. A football and cricket team consists of 11 players each. However simple the task in technological terms, the span of control of a team leader should probably not exceed ten or twelve people. This refers to the number who are directly responsible to any given leader, and who therefore constitute his team.

A good leader delegates

To delegate means to give a team member the authority and freedom to handle certain matters on his or her own initiative, with the confidence that they can do the job successfully. It is not to be confused with abdication of responsibility.

Delegation	Telling a team member the results required and giving them the authority – 'Do it your way and ask for help if required.'
Abdication	Relinquishing responsibility for the job – 'Do it any way you like but don't ask for help if it goes wrong.'

Remember that you should not delegate unless you are willing to give the person concerned the necessary authority to do the job, matched with your supportive trust in him or her. Be available to discuss progress or help with any problems the subordinate cannot deal with themselves. Grip your desk hard and do not interfere!

Accept the fact that the job will be done differently from the way that you would have done it, but still fall within the bounds of success.

Such effective delegation serves a two-fold purpose: it frees you for constructive work on larger projects, and it is a necessary technique for furthering the growth and development of subordinates. Make sure that the person knows what results are expected of him or her and make them accountable for their performance.

Organizing yourself

Sure signs of whether or not you are capable of executing the function of organizing lie in your own life. A good indicator is whether or not you are good at organizing your own time. It is essential for the leader to make time to think, both about the present and the future. That means in the first place an awareness of the value of time and the economical use of it. 'Ask me for anything,' Napoleon would say, 'except for time.' He knew that he had only 24 hours a day like anyone else, but he used his time very much more effectively than most people.

One method of developing your awareness and skill in time management is to keep a detailed diary of how you are spending your time. Often this reveals that relatively little time is being given to the key activities of leadership and communication, let alone thinking about decisions or problems. People dropping in during the morning, chatting or drinking coffee, or indiscriminate attention to all your emails as they come in can take up half your time. At the end of the day you go home with that uncomfortable feeling that you have not really achieved anything.

Making time to think

What advice can be offered to a leader? He must discipline himself and lead a carefully regulated and ordered life. He must allow a certain amount of time for quiet thought and reflection; the best times are in the early morning, and in the evening. The quality, good or bad, of any action which is to be taken will vary directly with the time spent in thinking; against this, he must not be rigid; his decisions and plans must be adaptable to changing situations. A certain ruthlessness is essential, particularly with inefficiency and also with those who would waste his time. People will accept this, provided the leader is ruthless with himself . . .

Most leaders will find there is so much to do and so little time to do it; that was my experience in the military sphere. My answer to that is not to worry; what is needed is a quiet contemplation of all aspects of the problem, followed by a decision – and it is fatal to worry afterwards.

FIELD MARSHAL LORD MONTGOMERY

Here are some practical suggestions to help you to make the best use of your time at work. Check yourself against this ten-point programme once a month for the next six months.

1 **Develop a personal sense of time**

Do not rely on memory or assume that you know where your time goes. For one or two weeks keep a record. Become more aware of the value of your time and resolve to use it well.

2 Identify your longer-term goals and policies

The clearer you are about your longer-terms ends, the easier you will find it to identify your priorities. Policies are decisions about principles: they help you to make many daily decisions without having to waste too much time on them.

3 Make middle-term plans

You should be able to translate fluently *purpose* into *aims*, and *aims* into *objectives* (see Figure 5.1, page 91). Plan your work on aims and objectives in terms of opportunities and desired results, priorities and deadlines.

4 Plan the day

Make a list of what you want to do each day. Arrange it or mark it in some order of priority. Learn to say no, otherwise you will become merely the slave to the priorities of others.

5 Make best use of your best time

Your best time is when you do your best work. Where possible, always use it for important tasks. Have some planned quiet periods for creative thinking.

6 Organize your administrative work

Work out systems for handling paperwork, dealing with emails and making telephone calls, so that you do not fragment your day. Make administration your servant and not your master.

7 Manage meetings

Work out the agenda carefully, allotting time for each item. Start on time and end on time. Use your skills as a leader to make meetings both business-like and enjoyable.

8 Delegate effectively

Where possible, delegate as many administrative responsibilities as you can. The reason for doing so is to free yourself for exercising the kind of leadership that your position requires.

9 Make use of committed time

Committed time is time given over to specific purposes, such as travel. Use waiting time or travelling time to think, plan or read or make calls.

10 Manage your health

Time management is primarily about the *quality* of your time, not about its *quantity*. Follow common sense guidelines over sleep, diet, exercise and holidays.

CHECKLIST: ORGANIZING

Organizing is an important function in meeting all three areas of the Three Circles model. Check your organizing ability in the following areas.

GROUP	Yes	No
Is the size of the working group correct and are the right people working together?	☐	☐
Is there a need for sub-groups to be constituted?	☐	☐
Are there regular opportunities or procedures for genuine consultation with the group before taking decisions affecting them e.g. decisions relating to work plans and output, work methods and standards, work measurement and overtime working?	☐	☐

ORGANIZATION

Are you clear on the purpose of the organization and how the various parts of it work together to achieve that end? ☐ ☐

Is there an effective system for staffing the organization and training? Is there a fair dismissal procedure? ☐ ☐

Do you carry out regular surveys of the organization to check:

    the size of all working groups? ☐ ☐

    the number of leadership levels? ☐ ☐

    the growth of unnecessary complexity? ☐ ☐

    line and staff co-operation? ☐ ☐

    that the communication systems are working properly? ☐ ☐

YOURSELF

Are there ways in which you could organize your personal and working life, e.g. how you deal with your personal administration, in order to be a more effective leader? ☐ ☐

Do you delegate sufficiently? ☐ ☐

Have you identified at least three steps you can take in order to become a better organizer of your time?

1. ....

2. ....

3. ....

Key points

- **Organizing** is the function of arranging parts into a working order. 'Structure is a means for attaining the objectives and goals of an institution,' writes Peter Drucker. This is no more than another application of the Three Circles model.

- At *team level* you may have to organize for results by setting up **sub-groups**. At *organizational level*, however, the principle may mean introducing **structural changes** to respond to changes in the task, technology or the environment.

- The Three Circles model serves as a guide for carrying out your own survey of your own team structure. It is based upon common sense principles. Bringing about the changes will, of course, require considerable powers of leadership.

- To be effective as a leader you should be able to organize your own work. You should become especially good at managing your time, for it is your most precious resource. For you need time to think about time for other people.

- 'Time wasted is existence, used is life,' wrote the poet Edward Young. So it is worth recalling to yourself often that nothing belongs to you but your time, and you have it even if you have nothing else.

- Achieve a balance between work and private life that works for you and keeps you free from the toxic kinds of stress.

'It is not enough to be busy. The question is: What are you busy about?'

HENRY THOREAU

11

Evaluating

'If you can meet with triumph and disaster
And treat those two imposters just the same . . .'
RUDYARD KIPLING

Appraising, evaluating, reviewing, rating, assessing, judging and estimating are all aspects of the basic function of valuing. These ships can all sail here under the flagship of *evaluating:* the ability to determine or fix the value of something.

Like analysing and synthesizing, the other two basic functions of intelligence, valuing enters into all of a leader's thinking and action. The controlling function, for example, clearly involves some evaluating of progress against yardsticks or standards. In this section we shall concentrate on some specific skills which you will need to acquire or develop as a leader, namely:

- Assessing consequences

- Evaluating team performance

- Appraising and training individuals

- Judging people.

Assessing consequences

In all organizations there are some people who have a reputation for good judgement in the sense that they are adept at assessing the consequences of any potential action inside and outside the organization. Equally we all know people who lack judgement in this respect. In industry they are often responsible for triggering off strikes, stoppages or other breakdowns in industrial relations.

In the decision-making or problem-solving process you will have to assess the consequences of proposed courses of action or solutions before making up your mind. It is helpful to bear in mind that consequences can be divided into six categories, which overlap considerably. These are described in Table 11.1.

Table 11.1 *Probing the consequences*

Type of consequence	Probing Questions
Desirable	What solid advantages does this course or solution have in terms of the common purpose, aim or objective?
Undesirable	Does it have unwelcome side-effects? Does it create more problems than it solves?
Manifest	What consequences – good or bad – are open to view now?
Latent	There will be consequences I cannot foresee now. Can I cut down their number by further thought or research? Have I sufficient resources to deal with possible contingencies?
Task	What are the technical consequences of adopting this method rather than that?
People	What will be the effects on (a) team (b) individuals (c) organization (d) society (e) myself?

In some instances you will be reduced to rough estimates or guesses about these consequences. But the greater the amount of science you bring to bear, the more you can predict consequences with accuracy. Where possible, turn estimates into calculations. In industry that means carrying out a rigorous cost/benefit evaluation of the courses open to you.

With regard to 'people' consequences, a matter of vital concern to the leader, a common mistake is to guess instead of finding out by going and asking the people concerned. 'They will never agree to working extra shifts, that's for sure. They never have done in the past,' said a board director. But that is an unexamined assumption. (Remember Exercise 5 – the dots and matchsticks!) Test that consequence to see if it is a real one – you may get a pleasant surprise.

Someone once neatly summed up the decision-making process as being in three phases: **making the decision**, **implementing it** and **living with the consequences**. The latter divide into two forms at the point where you are deciding: **manifest** – plainly apparent or obvious at the time; and **latent** – hidden or concealed to the decision-maker.

You can develop your ability to assess those consequences in advance – except for the latent ones – by carefully analysing cause-and-effect in what happens. Gradually you identify patterns or tendencies. It becomes easier to predict what will happen. Your 'depth mind' – the subconscious centre or most of your ten thousand million brain cells – can sometimes act as a computer in this respect, printing out warnings, judgements or expectations. An informed or educated depth mind, fed upon experience analysed and digested, is a valuable asset for any leader.

A leader's private computer

'If I have any advice to pass on, it is this: if one wants to be successful, one must think until it hurts. One must worry a problem in one's mind until it seems there cannot be another aspect of it that hasn't been considered. Believe me, that is hard work and, from my close observation, I can say that there are few people indeed who are prepared to perform this arduous and tiring work.

But let me go further and assure you of this: while, in the early stages, it is hard work and one must accept it as such, later one will find that it is not so difficult, the thinking apparatus has become trained; it is trained even to do some of the thinking subconsciously. The pressure that one had to use on one's poor brain in the early stages no longer is necessary; the hard grind is rarely needed; one's mental computer arrives at decisions instantly or during a period when the brain seems to be resting. It is only the rare and most complex problems that require the hard toll of protracted mental effort.'

ROY THOMSON, *After I was Sixty* (1975)

Evaluating team performance

In working enterprises it is often valuable to have a de-briefing session after a particular project. This gives you the chance to evaluate the performance of the group as a whole in relation to the task. First you should have a realistic and honest statement of results in terms of the following:

Success	Objectives all achieved.
Limited success	Some objectives or part of an objective attained but not others.
Failure	None of the objectives achieved.

Then you should move on to the evaluation proper. You can either initiate this phase by giving your own views, or invite comments from the team as a whole. Unless you are a very experienced leader, it is best always to follow the simple drill of identifying the good points first – what went well – and then coming on to the points for improvement. These should include constructive ways in which the team performance as a whole can be changed for the better. You may take decisions on the spot to effect these changes or choose to think about it for a day or two.

Group meetings for de-briefing purposes are usually not the right place to deal with individual failings unless you want to make an example of someone for the benefit of the group as a whole.

At de-briefing meetings, however, you can tackle any particular problems that have caused the group to fragment into independent rather than inter-dependent parts. The film *Twelve O'Clock High* provides a good illustration of the latter. During one de-briefing meeting, while the 918 Bomb Group is still sustaining heavy losses over enemy territory, Savage finds that some individuals are putting their close friends first.

Savage: Pettigill!

Pettigill: Yes, Sir.

Savage: We were plenty lucky to have only one loss on this strike. Why did you break formation?

Pettigill: Well, Sir, Ackermann was in trouble, two engines on fire, and we were getting enemy fighters. I figured I'd better stay back with him and try to cover him going into the target. But he couldn't make it.

Savage: (after a pause): Ackermann a pretty good friend of yours?

Pettigill: My room-mate Sir.

Savage So for the sake of your room-mate, you violated Group integrity. Every gun on a B.17 is designed to give the Group maximum defensive fire-power, that's what I mean by Group integrity. When you pull a B.17 out of formation you reduce the defensive power of the Group by ten guns. A crippled aeroplane has to be expendable. The one thing which is never expendable is your obligation to this Group. This Group, this Group, that has to be your loyalty, your only reason for being! Stovall!

Stovall: Yes, Sir

Savage: Have the Billeting Officer work out a complete reassignment of quarters so that every man has a new room-mate.

Stovall: Very well, Sir.

In this scene Savage shows considerable skill, which is worth exploring further. He *senses* a problem and asked a *probing question* to complete his diagnosis: 'Ackermann a pretty good friend of yours?' He *orders* the re-allocation of rooms to deal with what he has diagnosed as a *general problem*, and he *reiterates the group standard* he is trying to set: in this case putting the group first and self second.

Appraising and training individuals

'Appraisal meeting' is a familiar term in management jargon. This is a regular interview, sometimes as little as once a year, when a manager sits down with his or her subordinate and appraises the work of the subordinate against their objectives. 'Don't tell me that the man is doing good work,' said Andrew Carnegie to one of his plant bosses. 'Tell me what good work he is doing.'

During an appraisal meeting you should create an environment where you can have a constructive dialogue with a subordinate (or superior or colleague for that matter) on the following agenda:

- Past performance

- Future work to be done, targets, priorities, standards and strategies

- Matching perceptions of what each can reasonably expect from the other

- Improving skills, knowledge and behaviour.

Table 11.2 *Performance appraisal interviewing*

PERFORMANCE APPRAISAL INTERVIEWING	
Guidelines	**Notes**
1 Ensure the necessary data is available	To substantiate discussion and to keep it factual, all documents, reports, data or back-up information should be readily available for the interview.
2 Put the other person at ease	Both parties should try to be relaxed, open minded, aware of the purpose of the meeting, committed to its purpose and be prepared to discuss things calmly and frankly.
3 Control pace and direction of interview	Both parties have a part to play to control and influence the pace and direction of the interview to keep it relevant, helpful and work-orientated.

4	Listen ... listen ... listen	The most difficult part of the interview is for both parties to really listen to each other. Listening is more than not speaking, it is emptying the mind of preconceived ideas or prejudices. It is being willing to consider another person's point of view and if that view is better than the one previously held, being humble enough – and big enough – to accept it.
5	Don't be destructively critical	Where possible, people should be encouraged to be self-critical – critical of their own performance and motivated to improve. This approach goes a long way to remove the unnecessary conflict from the meeting.
6	Review performance systematically	It is important to stick to the facts – facts which can be substantiated – and that's where the relevant back-up information comes in handy.
7	Discuss future action	This is an opportunity to discuss with one another – almost on equal terms – what has been done, how it can best be done, who will do it, when, and to what standard.
8	Be prepared to discuss potential or aspirations	The question of the individual's potential for future promotion doesn't always arise, but it is wise to be prepared for it.
9	Identify essential training/ development required	The final part of the interview is usually devoted to discussing the training and counselling which may be required in order to carry out the agreed action plan.
10	Avoid obvious pitfalls	Such things as: • talking too much and hogging the conversation • introducing unnecessary conflict • jumping to hasty conclusions • unjustly blaming others – particularly those who are not present to defend themselves • expecting the impossible – like wanting a person to change significant character traits overnight • lastly, making promises which neither party may be able to keep.

Table 11.2 contains some guidelines which you may find useful to both the roles of being an appraiser and of being appraised.

At the end of the meeting or shortly afterwards, any agreed future actions should be written down. What has to be done? When? To what standard?

Do not expect too much from a system of formal performance appraisal meetings. Certainly, if they are not followed up by action from both the appraiser and the appraisee, they can soon degenerate into empty rituals. But the results of a good appraisal, when linked with good counselling, include better teamwork, improved commitment and the development of knowledge, skill and character.

On-the-job training

General Horrocks recalled one incident which revealed Montgomery's ability to develop the individual, even at the higher levels of leadership.

'On the day after the battle [Alam Halfa] I was sitting in my headquarters purring with satisfaction. The battle had been won and I had not been mauled in the process. What could be better? Then in came a liaison officer from 8th Army headquarters bringing me a letter in Monty's even hand. This is what he said:

"Dear Horrocks,

Well done – but you must remember that you are now a corps commander and not a divisional commander . . ."

He went on to list four or five things which I had done wrong, mainly because I had interfered too much with the

tasks of my subordinate commanders. The purring stopped abruptly.

Perhaps I wasn't quite such a heaven-sent general after all. But the more I thought over the battle, the more I realized that Monty was right. So I rang him up and said, "Thank you very much."

I mention this because Montgomery was one of the few commanders who tried to train the people who worked under him. Who else, on the day after his first major victory, which had altered the whole complexion of the war in the Middle East, would have taken the trouble to write a letter like this in his own hand to one of his subordinate commanders?'

LIEUT. GENERAL SIR BRIAN HORROCKS,
A Full Life (1956)

Therefore, you should see the formal system as at best a safety net for a process that should be going on continually. As the leader, you should be continually assessing the value of each individual's contribution and giving him or her feedback on how they are doing. Sometimes individuals, especially the over-modest ones, may genuinely undervalue some action or function they perform. It is a kind of occupational inferiority complex. The leader can correct this misjudgement. He or she may also, as we have seen, have occasions to point out the shortfalls in objectives.

However, a leader is not in the seat of a judge in the law court impartially appraising someone's actions while they stand in the dock. He or she is out to improve performance. Leaders have to be skilled in communicating both their perceptions of the strengths and the weaknesses of the individual concerned. They must have data or information at hand to back up any observation they give.

Above all, they must put their suggestions across so that they are acceptable and actionable by the individual. The best way to do that is to ask the individual to appraise his or her own performance against standing or continuing aims and specific objectives. Then agree with them an action plan for the future.

Thus, the function of appraising an individual's performance is only useful if it is the prelude to some form of learning or training. Even if the result of the interview is that you dismiss that person, or transfer him to another group, it can still be presented in a positive light as a lesson you have learned together. As a leader you need to be in part a teacher or trainer of people. Conversely, a teacher has to be something of a leader.

It is possible to teach yourself specific techniques, such as asking questions of different kinds which may be useful in appraisal meetings. The following could be useful examples:

Opening	'Tell me about your sales programme.'
Probing	'Is that the first time you failed to meet a target?'
Factual	'Where were you when it happened?'
Reflective	'You obviously feel very disappointed and upset at what was said to you.'
Leading	'I suppose you will improve that next year?'
Limited choice	'If you had to choose between general recruitment work and specializing in employment law, which would it be?'

What matters more, however, is to take seriously your responsibilities for developing the individual as his or her mentor throughout the year, not just for an hour or two in a formal or semi-formal meeting. You should be able to offer each individual person something drawn from your practical wisdom.

Unfortunately, unless your subordinate appraises *you* highly in that respect, he or she is unlikely to want to learn from you. As Winston Churchill once remarked to his wife, 'I cannot stand being taught – but I enjoy learning.' What is it in you that might make people want to learn from you? Given that you have a modicum of wisdom, it is best to see yourself not as a coach training a sportsman, but as a more experienced artist sitting down beside another and commenting helpfully on the work in hand.

Remember Cicero's definition of an orator: 'a good man skilled in speaking'. The development of another person may well test your goodness as well as your skill as a teacher. For practical wisdom consists of intelligence, experience and goodness. But mentoring is one of those activities that can make leadership such a rewarding experience.

Judging people

You may hear it said about some leaders who are outstanding in other respects: 'He is no judge of character. Some of the appointments he has made have been disastrous.'

Conversely some people – not all leaders – have a natural flair for forming accurate judgements about people and how they are likely to behave in certain situations. If you have some natural ability as a judge you can develop it by observation, experience and study. It is especially instructive to check appointments made by others in your organization against your own knowledge of that person on the one hand and the requirements of the job on the other. Would you have made that appointment? Did it turn out to be a good, average or weak decision in terms of results?

The practice of having favourites is a dangerous one for leaders on several scores. First, it breaks up team unity. Research has shown that, if an Arctic traveller makes a favourite of one husky among his sledge dogs, the effectiveness of the whole team sharply deteriorates. Secondly, the person you have chosen as your favourite is seen by others as an example of your judgement about people. If others, who know their colleagues better than you do, fail to agree upon your apparently high estimate of your favourite's worth, then your credibility suffers. Thirdly, favourites advance by astutely recognizing and pandering to the social and esteem needs of their bosses. If they sense that you like flattery, they will lay it on with a trowel. Some people are natural courtiers and will vie for your favour with such gifts. In time your judgement can become impaired and you may forget the trivial reasons why you have patronized them – such as their charm or amusing conversation – and you may actually promote them into responsible positions, where they will surely fail.

Assuming that you have remained impartial and even-handed (although it is only human to like some people more than others), the best way to improve your judgements and decisions about people is to take them slowly and work harder at them. There should be times when you actively work on the question by analysing your impressions and discussing them with others, followed by times when you relegate the matter to your subconscious or 'depth mind' for further resolution.

People decisions

Among the effective executives I have had occasion to observe, there have been people who make decisions fast, and people who make them rather slowly. But without exception, they made personnel decisions slowly and they make them several times before they really commit themselves.

Alfred P Sloan, Jr., former head of General Motors, the world's largest manufacturing company, was reported never to make a personnel decision the first time it came up. He made a tentative judgment, and even that took several hours as a rule. Then, a few days or weeks later, he tackled the question again, as if he had never worked on it before. Only when he came up with the same name two or three times in a row was he willing to go ahead. Sloan had a deserved reputation for the 'winners' he picked. But when asked about his secret, he is reported to have said: 'No secret – I have simply accepted that the first name I come up with is likely to be the wrong name – and I therefore retrace the whole process of thought and analysis a few times before I act.' Yet Sloan was far from a patient man.

Few executives make personnel decisions of such impact. But all effective executives I have had occasion to observe have learned that they have to give several hours of continuous and uninterrupted thought to decisions on people if they hope to come up with the right answer.

PETER DRUCKER, *The Effective Executive* (1967)

Self-evaluation

Like the other functions, you can apply the principle of evaluating to yourself and your work. Indeed, one major objective for you is to form a clear vision of what *excellence* in leadership means. Then you can appraise your progress in the light of it at regular intervals. For the best way to learn leadership is to do your present job as well as possible and to carefully monitor your own performance. If you can develop the insight to monitor your leadership performance, then even mistakes and failures will disclose positive lessons.

In this context you should always evaluate yourself in relation to the generic role – the responsibilities and functions of leadership. Leadership is an other-centred activity, not a self-centred one, and therefore you should avoid any form of self-preoccupation.

'We have to consider our responsibilities. We are to regard the duties of which we are capable, but not our capabilities simply considered. There is to be no complacent self-contemplation. When the self is viewed, it must always be in the most intimate connection with its purposes.'

WILLIAM GLADSTONE, *former UK Prime Minister*

Learn from your mistakes

There is one contingency that you need to think about in advance – **failure**. You will certainly encounter it in the exercise of leadership, for there can be no great **success** unless you are willing sometimes to work on the edge of failure.

Using the Three Circles model and the rest of this book, work hard to diagnose the *cause* of that failure. It may have lain within you, or in circumstances beyond your control. But you need to know. So you must ruthlessly track down the cause of failure as if you were investigating an aeroplane crash. You will not regain your confidence to fly again until you understand what went wrong and know that you have mended the fault in yourself or in the team. As Emerson said, 'A man's success is made up of failures, because he experiments and ventures every day, and the more falls he gets, moves faster on... I have heard that in horsemanship he is not the good rider who never was thrown, but rather that a man will never be a good rider until he is thrown; then he will not be haunted any longer by the terror that he shall tumble, and will ride whither he is bound.'

Thus, failure can be your best teacher. It can also give you the priceless gift of humility. As the vice-president of an American company once said to me, 'I have had enough success to keep me from despair, and enough failure to keep me humble.'

How to learn from feedback

Feedback is simply information that comes to you about people's reactions – in this case, positive or negative reactions to your performance in the generic role of *leader* as it is embedded in your job.

Don't worry: there will always be plenty of feedback. You shouldn't have to go out of your way to solicit it – just keep your ears and eyes open. Personally, I am against the practice of setting up managerial systems to solicit feedback. In the first place, it sends out the signal of self-centredness; in the second place, there is really no need – it is always there. If you don't know what your team, colleagues or boss think of you, it's no good sending them a questionnaire!

Remember that all the fragments of feedback that come your way are only **personal impressions**: no one has a window into your soul – not even you. But the impressions that others form of you are nonetheless facts. Of course, some people will know you better than others and may be more perceptive. Feedback needs to be sifted before it is taken on board, but beware of dismissing the more critical reactions to your leadership by some form of self-indulgent rationalization.

The principle is to look for a pattern in the feedback from superiors, colleagues or subordinates – solicited or unsolicited – that comes your way. There's a Hungarian saying:

When a man says you are a horse laugh at him.
When two men assert that you are a horse, give it a thought.
And when three men say you are a horse, you had better go and buy a saddle for yourself.

If you know the general impression you are giving – be it in the domain of qualities, knowledge or functions – you have the freedom to change your behaviour. Painful as it may be at the time, although it is usually from stinging critical feedback that we learn the most, we come to know that it is only through the eyes of others can we see our faults. And in time we can appreciate that this painful self-knowledge is a kind of blessing. As the Arabs say: *When God wishes a man well, he gives him insight into his faults.*

CHECKLIST: EVALUATING

In assessing the outcome of possible courses of action or solutions, do you take time to consider the consequences for the team and the individual as well as the task?

Always ☐   Sometimes ☐   Rarely ☐

How would you assess yourself as an appraiser or evaluator of the work of your team and of each individual team member?

Good   You hold regular evaluation meetings and do   ☐
quite a lot on a day-to-day basis. You always
support general points with evidence. You tend
always to praise first and criticize second. Your
appraising usually results in better work
performance.

Average   Sometimes it seems to work, other times not.   ☐
You find it difficult to hit the right note with
some people. Quite frankly, awkward people,
who don't want to learn, defeat you.

Weak   You lose credibility every time you try to   ☐
appraise someone. It usually ends up in an
argument. You tell them, but they refuse to listen.

What is your record in judging people? In selecting and promoting individuals, which of the following statements characterizes your approach?

You can always pick a winner, and never consult anyone   ☐
else or seek specialist advice.

You go by first impressions. Even if you think you are   ☐
wrong you usually return to them in the end.

You take people decisions slowly. You like to consult ☐
others who know the person, often on a confidential basis.
You do not trust your own first thought.

You like to see a person in a variety of different situations ☐
before making up your mind. Track record is an important
factor to you, more so than psychological tests and the like.

You rarely choose a person on technical grounds alone, ☐
unless he or she is working on his or her own. You try to
see them in the context of being a team leader or member,
and judge if they will get on well with the individuals in
that group.

Would you regard your regular evaluation of your own
performance as (a) more rigorous (b) less searching or
(c) about the same as your evaluation of others?

(a) ☐   (b) ☐   (c) ☐

Key points

- When people have worked hard at any task, they need to have
  their work fairly and professionally evaluated. How else can
  they learn to do better next time?

- The ability to evaluate is an important leadership function.
  In this chapter it has been discussed under four headings:
  *assessing consequences, evaluating team performance,
  appraising and training individuals* and *judging people.*

- A crucial element in decision making is evaluating the
  alternatives in terms of their consequences – technical,
  financial and human.

- Unless you can **evaluate team performance** with skill, the people working for you will miss a vital part of the feedback which should be coming their way. The better the team, the more it aspires to excellence, the more it welcomes constructive criticism.

- Appraising the **contribution of individuals** is a continuous activity, part of the process of calling forth the best from people.

- The higher you have risen as a leader, the more important it is for you to develop good **judgement about people**. Avoid having favourites. The test of your ability in this respect lies in the performance of the people you have appointed. 'By their fruits you shall know them.'

Those who are near will not hide their ability, and those
Who are distant will not grumble at their toil . . . That is

   What is called being a leader and teacher of men.

HSÜ TZU

12

Leading by example

'The lantern carrier should go ahead.'

JAPANESE PROVERB

As a leader, you cannot help setting an example – the question is whether it will be a good or a bad one. If you are setting a good example the people will tend not to be too aware of it, but they will certainly notice and comment upon a bad example.

The Russians have a saying, '*Nothing is so contagious as a bad example*.' This is something long remarked upon by wise men. Francis Bacon said: 'He that gives good advice builds with one hand. He that gives good counsel and example builds with both. But he that gives good admonition and bad example, builds with one hand and pulls down with the other.' There you have it.

Example is important, then, because people take in information more through their eyes than their ears. Hence the proverb *A picture is worth a thousand words*. When you take on the role of leader, you become the picture!

For what they see you do is far more powerful than what they hear you say. The basic principle is that the word and example should always go together – they should support each other. If they conflict, you must expect people to follow your example and not your precept. 'Don't do as I do – do as I say' – those words should never pass the lips of a true leader, except in so far as they acknowledge that he or she is aspiring towards a common high standard, and, being human, is all too aware of their own shortcomings. People will respect you if you try to set the right example, even if you fall short on occasion.

We all know from experience the power of the example of others on our own motivation. If a leader is enthusiastic and motivated it is contagious.

Exercise 7

Can you identify any leader who has inspired or motivated you?

What characteristics did they have?

Conversely, can you think of an incident where a bad example set by a manager reduced the energy and motivation of the group?

Many managers, if they were honest, would have to admit they are like the character in Shakespeare's *Merchant of Venice* who declared: 'I can easier teach twenty what were good to be done, than be one of the twenty to follow my own teaching.'

Perhaps it is best to think of example as something you provide rather than set. Setting an example suggests a conscious intention to do something for effect. Shouldn't example spring out of what you are and what you believe, regardless of effect?

You may disagree with me that good example shouldn't be consciously calculated. But in my experience doing things for effect can be counter-productive. In this context it's a fairly academic point, because you can't *simulate* energetic purposefulness, enthusiasm or drive. If those around you are to see and feel it in you, then it has to be really there.

Table 12.1 *Hallmarks of good example*

Spontaneous	Example is best when it is perceived as spontaneous, not calculated. Let it happen naturally.
Expressive	Leadership should be *you*. Don't do things for effect – do them because it's natural for you. Why does the bird sing?
Self-effacing	Good example shouldn't draw attention to itself. It is not self-seeking. No trumpets!

In the task area

A root meaning of *leadership* is leading in the sense of literally going out in front of others. The original Old English verb is only found in the *causative* tense. It means to *cause* people to follow you – freely, of their own accord. An Alpine guide, for example, may show some followers in what direction they should be travelling.

When we widen the reference of leading by example to non-physical situations, the leader is still the person who causes others to move forward freely by their example. Leadership implies the personal willingness to go out in front – accepting the risks involved – in order to ensure that your team go in the right direction at the right speed and with a willing heart.

Leading from the front

**Napoleon's presence on the battlefield inspired confidence in his
soldiers and the will to fight. As they formed up at Austerlitz on
the cold, misty morning of December 2, 1805, he promised his
soldiers: 'I shall direct every one of your battalions myself ...
but if for one instant, victory should look uncertain, you shall
behold your Emperor expose himself in the front rank.'**

**Equally conspicuous in sharing the dangers of the front line
were his generals, who led from the front and set examples of
fearlessness. Mortally wounded, General Valhubert refused to
leave the field, declaring to his men: 'I will die just as well here.'
He did and they fought on; valour was contagious.**

To continue the analogy, if you are too far ahead of the group – too
advanced in your thinking – you run the risk of losing contact with
them altogether. If you are too far behind, however, you may find
yourself saying, like a politician in the French Revolution of 1848 who
was trying to force his way through a mob of which he was one of the
chief instigators, 'Let me pass, I have to follow them, I am their leader.'

Just how much of an example you should set by personally doing
the work yourself depends upon your level of leadership. At the lower
levels you should expect to lead by doing the job yourself – or part of
it at least – in the way you expect it to be done. But the other functions
of leadership, notably controlling and co-ordinating, should take
priority if there is any conflict over how your time should be spent.

In the military field this aspect of leadership tends to be crystal
clear. The platoon commander is expected to lead his platoon from
the front; the squadron leader flies his own fighter as well as controlling

the squadron. At a certain level, however, the military commander does not lead the attack in person. 'We shall be right behind you on the day, sir' said one eager sergeant to General Slim in Burma in the Second World War. 'Make no mistake, Sergeant,' replied Slim with a smile, 'when the day comes you will be several miles in front of me!'

Does the senior leader then stop leading by example? Not necessarily. The fact that he or she at some stage in their careers has led 'from the front' in the basic task is itself an important factor in winning the respect of their younger colleagues at all levels. It has the added practical advantage that people know such a leader will not ask them to do what he or she would not be willing to do themselves – or to have done in the past. If the leader is not willing to do the job themselves, they can hardly command others to do it.

Ask not of others . . .

At the age of twenty-one, I was working as a deckhand on a Hull fishing trawler. The mate in charge of the deckhands was a large bully of a man with a chip on his shoulder, for he had recently been a skipper but lost his ticket through incompetence.

One afternoon, in a winter storm near Iceland, he told one of the men to shin up the mast and adjust an unsafe navigation light. 'Not bloody likely,' said the man, looking at the kicking mast and hissing waves. 'You do it, Bill,' thundered the mate to another deckhand. 'Not me,' replied Bill with a shrug. The mate began to shout and swear at us all.

Attracted by the commotion on deck, the skipper came down from the bridge. 'What's up?' he asked. The mate told him. 'Why

don't you go up yourself?' the skipper said to the mate, looking him in the eye. Silence. 'Right, I'll do it myself,' said the skipper, and began to pull off his oilskin. He meant it too. At once three or four men stepped forward and volunteered, for we had no desire to lose our navigator overboard.

Which was the true leader – the mate or the skipper?

Even at the more senior levels of leadership it is sometimes possible for the leader to give what might be called a symbolic example. When Napoleon found a sentry asleep one night he took up the man's musket and stood guard himself for a few hours. Occasionally a senior leader can 'lend a hand', working beside his people for an hour or two.

Such gestures can have an electric effect upon subordinates, in direct proportion to the rank or seniority of the leader concerned. The grapevine, which can be a positive as well as a negative factor in large organizations, will carry the good news around. When Julius Caesar, their Commander-in-Chief, sat around a mess table with ten soldiers of a Roman legion sharing their meal of bread, meat and rough wine and then in the afternoon took part in their military exercises, the whole Roman Army had heard about it within a few weeks.

Leadership involves the ability to inspire, and people are touched by such imaginative gestures. A gram of example is worth a kilogram of exhortation. Sometimes such a symbolic act can serve to remind a group or an organization of the basic meaning of leadership. It is as if the leader is saying 'I should like to be with you all more often, especially when there is a dirty or arduous job to be done, but my other responsibilities just do not allow me to. At least what I have done this afternoon is a token that I mean what I say.'

In team and individual circles

The importance of setting an example in establishing, maintaining, or altering group standards has been touched upon already. Whatever you require the group to do, you should be prepared to do yourself. Punctuality is an obvious instance. If you want each member to help the others with their work, you can best convey that by doing it yourself. The norms of human relations – listening, respecting, communicating and caring – can all be best conveyed by example.

When Jesus wanted to impress upon his disciples that as leaders they should be prepared to meet the needs of individuals, he did not give them a long lecture on social psychology. Instead he took a bowl, jug of water and a towel, knelt down and washed their dusty feet. By thus performing the functions of a lowly household servant, he was also teaching them the need for humility as leaders, a virtue in stark contrast to the domineering arrogance of many of the kings of the day.

'It is certain,' wrote Shakespeare in *King Henry IV*, 'that either wise bearing or ignorant carriage is caught, as men take diseases, therefore let men take heed of their company.' Example is contagious. It is action or conduct which induces imitation. Children are naturally imitative: it is the way they learn. As adults we retain that characteristic. In creating the right climate of purpose, unity and teamwork, how you bear yourself as leader can be decisive.

'You mention integrity as an important quality,' a manager asked Lord Slim at a large conference for managers and directors. 'Can you suggest how this quality can be spread in industry?' 'Yes, by example,' replied Slim.

Good example, then, has creative power, especially if it involves an element of self-sacrifice. It can work in people's minds to alter their ways. That process may take time, but the leader whose example backs up his words puts him or herself in an unassailable position. No one can accuse them of hypocrisy, of preaching one thing and doing another.

That is what gave Nelson Mandela his unique moral authority as a leader – he shared the dangers, hardships and sufferings of his people. Long years of imprisonment on Robben Island enhanced his stature as a leader by example. It gave him greater power to inspire others – even some of his captors.

You can see now that the principle of leading by example is a challenging one, for it involves not only what you *do* but also who you *are* and how you choose to live. It reminds you that leadership can never be a thing apart from the rest of your life. In practical terms your own example is the most powerful weapon at your command.

As Dag Hammarskjöld, Secretary General of the United Nations until 1961, wrote to himself one night in his diary: 'Your position never gives you the right to command. It only imposes on you the duty of so living your life that others can receive your orders without being humiliated.' Not long after he wrote those words, Hammarskjöld lost his life when the aircraft he was in crashed. He was on his way to try to bring peace to a troubled area in central Africa.

> 'These are hard times in which a genius would wish to live.
> Great necessities call forth great leaders.'
> ABIGAIL ADAMS, *writing to Thomas Jefferson, 1790*

CHECKLIST:
LEADING BY EXAMPLE

Which of these statements would you say most applies to you:

People often comment on the good example you set in your work. ☐

You never ask others to do what you are not willing to do yourself. ☐

Sometimes your bad example conflicts with all that we are trying to do here. ☐

You are not really aware of the importance of example and are unable to say what kind of one you are giving. ☐

On what occasion in the last month have you deliberately set out to give a lead by your example?

Did your action have any effect on the group or individual?
(a) Immediately   Yes ☐   No ☐
(b) Some days later   Yes ☐   No ☐

What specific problems in the team maintenance area might you help to solve by giving a better personal example yourself?
1.
2.

	Yes	No
Have you ever shared in the dangers, labours or hardships of those who look to you for leadership?	☐	☐

Key points

- Always remember that real leadership is done from in front. To do so not only shows the way; it causes others to go with you willingly.

- Example is all-important in teambuilding. It is not an easy path. Most of us can echo Shakespeare's words in *The Merchant of Venice*: 'I can easier teach twenty what were good to be done, than to be one of the twenty to follow my own teaching.'

- Real leaders share in the fortunes of their people, not claiming any special privileges or exemptions. They are among their people, not over them – servants rather than masters.

- You lead only where you are willing to go yourself. Where that physical leading is not appropriate you can set an example, for instance by working hard or being accurate and well informed.

- Example can help you to *build the team*, for you can illustrate by example the group standards you are seeking to maintain or alter for the better. The *individual* who knows you or sees you from afar may be inspired to emulate you.

- You may need some creative imagination to apply this principle of leading by example, but apply it you must if you are committed to becoming a better leader. If it calls for an element of self-denial or sacrifice on your part, so that you share fully in the dangers and hardships of your people, so much the better. That will almost certainly win a positive response.

Ducere est servire (To lead is to serve)

Motto of Britain's Chartered Management Institute

APPENDIX

Answers to exercises

Exercise 2: Have you got what it takes for a top job in leadership? (page 23)

Ranking of attributes rated most valuable at top level of management by a cross section of successful chief executives.

1 Ability to take decisions	13 Enterprise
2 Leadership	14 Capacity to speak lucidly
3 Integrity	15 Astuteness
4 Enthusiasm	16 Ability to administer efficiently
5 Imagination	17 Open-mindedness
6 Willingness to work hard	18 Ability to 'stick to it'
7 Analytical ability	19 Willingness to work long hours
8 Understanding of others	20 Ambition
9 Ability to spot opportunities	21 Single-mindedness
10 Ability to meet unpleasant situations	22 Capacity for lucid writing
	23 Curiosity
11 Ability to adapt quickly to change	24 Skill with numbers
12 Willingness to take risks	25 Capacity for abstract thought

Exercise 5: Creative solutions (page 102)

1   Many people unconsciously place a framework around the dots. They are making an assumption without realizing it. But the problem can only be solved by going outside those invisible, self-imposed barriers, thus:

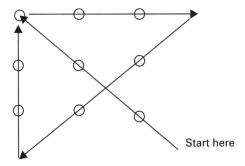

Start here

2   With the six matchsticks, too, people try to solve the problem in two dimensions. The most elegant solution, however, is to break that assumption and build a three-dimensional pyramid. A 'Star of David' arrangement is also acceptable. It involves some creativity, because you are at least putting matchsticks on top of each other, but it is less exciting.

INDEX

Page numbers in **bold** refer to figures, page numbers in *italic* refer to tables.